FRIDTJOF NANSEN

THROUGH THE CAUCASUS
TO THE VOLGA

Translated by

G. C. WHEELER

ILLUSTRATED

D1736423

NEW YORK

W · W · NORTON & COMPANY, INC

Publishers

DR. NANSEN

From a sketch made at Geneva, 1929

PREFACE

The journey described in this book was made in the summer of 1925, and was the continuation of the one described in an earlier book, *Armenia and the Near East (Gjennem Armenia)*. The author gladly uses this opportunity to express his gratitude to Presidents Samursky and Korkmazov in the Republic of Daghestan for the extraordinary hospitality shown to his fellow-traveller and himself during their interesting stay in this remarkable land.

He would also like to thank the local authorities in the different places they came to, especially in Astrakhan, for their friendly welcome.

It is not possible in a short sketch such as this to give in any way complete impressions of the lands and the many peoples the journey took them through, especially when it was made so quickly, and the impressions were so changing and over-whelming. For fuller information as to the natural conditions and the manifold peoples in the Caucasus and Daghestan the reader may be referred to the following among others: Erckert, *Der Kaukasus und seine Völker*, 1887; Merzbacher, *Aus den Hochregionen des Kaukasus*, 1901; Freshfield, *The Exploration of the Caucasus*, 1902; the various descriptions of travels by C. Hahn (*Aus dem Kaukasus*, 1892, and others in 1896, 1900, and 1911). A good account of our knowledge of the anthropology and customs of the

5

Caucasian peoples will be found in Arthur Byhan, "Die kaukasischen Völker" (in Buschan, *Illustrierte Völkerkunde*, vol. ii, part 2, 1926).

The most important sources for the study of the Caucasian peoples' long-drawn-out fight for freedom against the Russians are the many Russian military reports from the campaigns, and the many Russian accounts of the course of the fighting and so on. It is mainly on these Russian printed sources that J. F. Baddeley based his work, *The Russian Conquest of the Caucasus*, 1908, which describes the struggle of the Daghestaners and the Chechens for freedom. As a result of the nature of these sources and the lack of sources from the other side, it is only to be expected that this valuable work, in part at least, should express the Russian outlook on the course of the fighting and the conditions in Daghestan, even though the author has tried his best to guard himself against this. Bodenstedt's account in *Die Völker des Kaukasus und ihre Freiheitskämpfe gegen die Russen*, 1855, seems, on the other hand, to be less coloured by a Russian point of view; but he did not have access to the rich Russian material we now have. Olaf Lange, *Kavkasus*, Copenhagen, 1891, gives an entertaining survey of Muridism and Daghestan's fight for freedom, mostly based, it is true, on Bodenstedt. The Pole, Lapinski (Tefik Bey), in his *Die Bergvölker des Kaukasus und ihr Freiheitskampf gegen die Russen*, 1863, gives an interesting description of the fighting by the Circassians and Abkhasians, and of his share in it.

These introductory words cannot be brought to an end without my hearty thanks to Captain Vidkum Quisling for his untiring kindness as a travelling companion, and for the valuable help he has given the author through his knowledge of Russian and his many-sided attainments.

FRIDTJOF NANSEN

Lysaker,
November 1929

CONTENTS

ILLUSTRATIONS

11

THROUGH THE CAUCASUS TO THE VOLGA

I

TIFLIS

TIFLIS

Our commission of five had been in Armenia, and on behalf of the League of Nations had been examining how far it would be possible to settle the Armenian refugees there from Turkish Armenia, who were now scattered over Europe and elsewhere. In the night of Thursday, 2nd of July, 1925, we were in the train on our way home from Erivan.

It was still dark, when towards morning the train pulled up with a violent jerk, and I heard people in the next compartment, where my fellow-commissioners were sleeping. They must get ready at once, they were told; the motor-cars were waiting to take them to Batum, and the train would not stop for long.

What was it all about? and where were we? We were in Leninakan, and motor-cars had indeed been ordered for Batum. The Frenchman, the lively Carle, was at once wide-awake and ready; it was he who had wired for cars. Dupuis, the Englishman, not yet quite awake, stood there in his underwear and protested loudly against this fuss; he knew nothing about it all, and would not hear of going by car. Young Lo Savio, the Italian, categorically refused, turned to the wall and went on sleeping; while our secretary, the Norwegian Quisling, who had not to go to Batum, took it all quite calmly.

The whole question was about the steamer from

Batum to Constantinople. Some days before we left Erivan it was announced to sail on the 6th of July, and we arranged our journey accordingly. Then a wire came that it was leaving on the 4th of July, so that they had just time to catch it. But when on the same day (2nd of July) we left Erivan, we had another wire to say it was sailing the very next day (3rd of July), so that there was no chance of catching it. I wired back to the steamship company that we were going by its earlier telegrams as to the time of sailing, putting the responsibility on them if my fellow-commissioners did not catch the boat, as there was not another one for several weeks. Meanwhile the active Carle had wired to Leninakan, and asked whether motor-cars could be had to take them over the mountains to Batum and catch the boat there on the 3rd of July. He had hoped to take his two colleagues at the same time; but in spite of their liking for any kind of adventure, he had to give it up now in the face of this sleepy laziness, and the train went on.

Reaching Tiflis in the morning, we found a telegram to say the boat was sailing next day. Captain Quisling and myself were to travel home through Russia, and in the afternoon we parted sorrowfully from our three good fellow-workers, who went on by train to Batum. We had spent some crowded weeks together, and believed we had done some good work. We two who were left behind thankfully accepted the friendly bidding of the Near East Relief to take up our quarters in its hospitable house while we were in Tiflis.

The world is not so very big: in this foreign town I was surprised to meet Mrs. Petrov, the daughter of my friend Wurzel, formerly director of works for the Imperial Russian railways; it was with him that I travelled through Siberia and the Amur district in 1913. She has lived many years in Tiflis with her husband, whose work is in insurance, especially for agriculture. I spent a delightful evening with them and their young and lovely daughter in their peaceful home. They had come fairly well through those anxious times, without having to undergo such sufferings as many others had to. They had been allowed to keep their furniture and four rooms, so comparatively they were not crowded. But otherwise the lack of housing was severely felt in Tiflis as in most of the greater towns of the Soviet Union, and many families had to put up with one room only. Mr. Petrov had travelled widely on account of his work both in Georgia and in Armenia, and had a good knowledge of the state of things in the various districts. Things had gone badly, too, with agriculture in those hard years during the war with the Turks and after, especially in Armenia, where the people had been put to the sword, the land had been laid waste and plundered, and the harvest destroyed time after time by the Turkish hordes; while there had also been the many thousands of harassed Armenian refugees pouring in an unbroken flood over the borders from Turkish Armenia. In the winter of 1921-2 men died in thousands from hunger; the bodies of the dead lay strewn in the streets of

Leninakan, Erivan, and other Armenian towns; but for there having been no heavy drought the conditions were in some ways as bad as they were in the hunger tracts of the Volga valley that winter. But under skilful management agriculture had now in great part recovered itself, although there was still much that could be bettered.

The Petrovs had a young son who was to be brought up as an engineer, like so many young Russians now; this is probably because the development of industry and the exploitation of the natural wealth of this vast land are looked upon as the great task set before the nation in the future. He was now one of those working on the great dam for a power station which is being built across the river Kura in the valley north of Tiflis.

I had to carry on negotiations with the Trans-Caucasian government in connection with the work of our commission in Armenia, and our proposal to raise a loan of about 17 million *kroner* for watering and cultivating tracts in Armenia which are now almost desert, and bringing Armenian refugees thither. Armenia, Georgia, and Azerbaidjan are three independent Soviet republics, each with its own government. They are united in a Trans-Caucasian federation under an administration made up of a vice-president for each republic, living in Tiflis. This federative republic, again, is united with the other Soviet socialist republics, under an administration in Moscow. The Armenian government in Erivan had given our proposal its full approval. I now discussed it with Lukashin, the

Armenian vice-president in the Trans-Caucasian government. The capable Armenian commissary for agriculture, Erzinkian, was also present. Lukashin was able to say that the Trans-Caucasian government was in agreement also, and to my joyful surprise he told me that it would have nothing to say against the loan being raised through the League of Nations. I had been afraid of difficulties on this point, for the Soviet governments will not recognize the League. He went on to say that the Trans-Caucasian government was ready, together with the Armenian government, to guarantee the redemption of the loan; and he believed that the Soviet government in Moscow and the Russian State Bank would also give their backing to this, if it were wished. With such guarantees as these there would be no difficulty in getting a loan on reasonable terms. I could not share his optimistic outlook on this point, and I had my fears that the European bankers would demand more concrete guarantees than general ones such as these, which might be thought likely to lose their value, should changes come about in the governments. Even though he might say that there was no likelihood of this, yet it was always a possibility which the banks would take into reckoning. I brought forward the great difficulties we had had to overcome when we were trying to raise a loan of the same kind for settling fugitives in Greece, in spite of the fact that the Greek state offered fixed guarantees and securities which in value were far greater than the sum to be raised. It had to be remembered that

19

banks are not beings with feelings and humanitarian aims; they are reckoning-machines, even if their working is not always perfect. I felt, therefore, that the whole task would be greatly lightened if specific guarantees could be given in the shape of definite securities or charges to be so made over as unconditionally to cover the loan whatever happened, and which should be under the control of the lenders. The simplest of all would have been for the tract itself which was brought under cultivation to be the security; but this was not possible, since all the land belonged to the state, and so could not be sold. Lukashin held that this plan would undoubtedly find great difficulties, and evidently could not see the need for it, nor that my fears were justified, when such a manifold guarantee was mutually given by the three governments, and by the State Bank of the mighty Soviet Union as well; it might be looked on as savouring of mistrust. I answered that of course there would be no lack of good will and earnestness on our side for bringing the business to a successful result, and that I only hoped he were right; but I could not hide from him that I foresaw great difficulties.[1] We parted from one another with the best mutual wishes.

[1] I am sorry to say my fears turned out only too well grounded; it was impossible to raise any loan for Armenia on the guarantees offered and without definite cover or security. On behalf of the banks the answer was made that my strong belief that the Armenian and the Soviet Moscow governments would be punctual payers was undoubtedly fully justified; but I wanted a loan which was to be paid back in fifteen years, and what could be guaranteed as to the conditions in these lands in fifteen years' time?

That evening our friend Narriman Ter Kasarian gave a dinner in the best hotel in the town. As the representative of the government of the Trans-Caucasian federation he had gone with us on the whole journey through Armenia and Georgia, and had been our host. I may say we called him Napoleon, owing to his likeness to Napoleon III. When at last the dinner began (some two hours after the time fixed), there was as usual a very well-laid table, with the choicest dishes and Caucasian wine. The vice-president of Georgia was there—a prominent Armenian who turned out to be a keen sportsman—and many others. All were in high spirits, and there were many lyrical speeches made to our commission and our undertaking, to Armenia, to Trans-Caucasia, to our kind friend Napoleon, and not least to fair Georgia. Of course, there was now a Soviet government here which looked down on all royalty, but notwithstanding this its proud history would come to mind once more, and its glories under the lovely queen Tamara. The Georgians had, indeed, always been admirers of woman's charm and knightly deeds; and this has found a wonderful utterance in Shota Rustaveli's poem, "The man in the tiger-skin", which after seven hundred years still lives on the lips of the nation.

After dinner we drove under a glorious moon by car up into the hills. We sat on the verandah of a restaurant and had nuts and wine. There were speeches and a good deal of merriment, much of which was aroused by the tales our Armenian friend told us of his many remarkable adventures. As an entertaining accompaniment we had a barrel-organ wonderfully out of tune, whose sounds came down to us with never a stop from the road beyond. We guessed that it was especially provided by our thoughtful host Napoleon. In the most melting parts of the melting melodies several notes had been lost, and this gave an irresistible effect. The notes that were still left were like teeth in a faulty set: their beauty was not heightened by the gaps.

Far below us along the Kura valley lay the town with its thousands of lights, the church towers lifted their silvery glistering domes above the house roofs; around us rose the hills one behind the other, bathed in moonlight. In the mist far away to the north were dimly felt the mighty ridges of the Caucasus.

Tiflis is a central point in this part of the world, and in it meet the manifold differing races of which this area is made up: Georgians, Armenians, Persians, Tatars, Kurds, Jews, Abkhasians, Cherkesses (Circassians), Chechens, Svanetians, Ossetes, Avars, and all the many other Caucasian mountain tribes. The result is a many-coloured picture of national types, from the stalwart, blond Kurds and Cherkesses to the dark Tatars, or the dark short-headed Avars and other Lesghis. It is in the old town, that is, the southern part of it, with its narrow streets and alleys, its bazaars, and the busy market, that this motley humanity can best be seen. Here the lively, enterprising Armenian seeks to make you take his goods for a price that may change again and again as you go your way and he follows you; while the dignified Persian sits stately on his crossed legs behind his own heap, and leaves it for you to decide whether you will agree to his price, which is certain not to be too low. It has been said that it takes four Jews to be a match for one Greek in trading, four Greeks to be a match for one Armenian, but four Armenians to match a Persian. Whether this is so may be left an open question, but anyhow the traders of this last nation are probably the most capable in the East. Here Persian and Caucasian carpets are on sale which might well tempt most weak mortals beyond endurance, were it not for the thought of the long journey by motor-car, train, and steamer to Norway. Farther on we come to streets with shops for goldsmiths' and silversmiths' work and for weapons, for which the Caucasus is renowned. The skilful Caucasian weapon-makers seek to convince you of the excellence of their weapons by striking the *kindjal* (the big Caucasian dagger) on the stones without any mark being left on the steel edge. Here too one may be surprised to see coats of mail offered for sale, and swords, iron-bound shields, and helmets, such as might well be relics from Crusading days, but which are still used by a few mountain tribes, especially the Khevsurs, high up in the remote Caucasian valleys.

The Caucasians' gold and silver work has been highly esteemed ever since olden times, especially the ornamental work of gold and silver inlaid in bone and steel. As their weapons always played so great a part in the whole life of the Caucasian mountain peoples, it was natural that this art of ornamentation should be particularly applied to weapons of all kinds, from *kindjals* and the smaller daggers up to muskets and pistols, powder-horns, shot-bags, and so forth. There were especially certain valleys and villages well known for their beautiful and well-made weapons. The craft seems now to have lost ground, but is still carried on.

Through the streets go the water-sellers; they call their precious fluid, which is carried in great leather bags on donkey- or horse-back; sometimes they carry it themselves. Water is an important article of trade in these towns, and particularly esteemed in the hot, dry summer, when there is not much of it. Boys with donkeys, heavily loaded with baskets of vegetables and fruit, also offer their wares.

What perhaps most strikes a stranger is the quiet seriousness which wraps all these people, in spite of the trading and bargaining, and the little show there is of any kind of joy in life; you hardly ever hear a refreshing laugh. Even the women here looked staid and serious, whether in the modern Russian quarter of the town or in the old Oriental quarter, where there are not so many of them to be seen now. In our part of the world, indeed, women are not wont to be so sparing of their voices. It is as though everywhere the music were played with mutes. Perhaps it is we European upstarts that do not know what dignity and good-breeding mean. It reminds me of what a Chinese diplomat once answered most undiplomatically to a journalist when he was asked what he thought about European civilization: "Well, it may be a good thing, if only it was not so cursedly noisy."

The houses in the older parts of the town are low, usually two-storied, with balconies or open galleries on the second floor; and on these the family, especially the women, spends the day, and often the night as well, in the heat of the year. They like to have at least two galleries and on different sides of each house, so that there is always one in the shade.

South of the old quarter of the town and the bazaars lie warm sulphur baths, which have been known and resorted to ever since olden times, and may have given the town its name: in Georgian, *Tbilis-Kalaki* (that is, the warm town).

A beautiful and peaceful spot in Tiflis is the Botanical Garden in a narrow valley on the high, steep hillside south of the town. It was refreshing to come from the burning heat of the day into the long, cool tunnel leading to the garden through the precipitous hill under the so-called Persian fort. The deep, narrow valley is cut into the hillside by the stream called Savkissi, which at this time was no more than a little trickling brook, but which evidently at times, when there have been heavy rains, may become a tearing, foaming stream, and make a high waterfall. The garden lies along the steep hillsides and the ground is romantically diversified, with a teeming, luxuriant vegetation made up of all kinds of southern trees and bushes.

In among them wound overgrown, shady paths on the hillsides. The remarkable thing is that nearly all the earth they grow in has been brought up to these ledges on the rock, and the whole is the work of busy human hands. Everywhere water was trickling down, led along small channels and courses; but on the other side of the valley there were stretches without water or trees, with brown, withered grass. An old ruined Mohammedan graveyard was to be seen over there, a reminder of what had once been, when Islam laid its strong grasp also on these oldest of Christian lands, which, ringed in and forsaken, were fighting their lone fight for faith and freedom. But Mohammed's arm has lost its strength; his time is over.

High up on the ridge of hills north of the garden stand the walls of the old "Persian" fort pointing to the sky. It lies at the edge of the precipice over the bazaars and warm baths of the town, looking far away over the valley and the Kura—which winds and falls in a gleaming yellow ribbon between the huddled houses of the town—and over the many glistening domes of the churches, and to the north as far as the blue mountain wall, with Kasbek's shining snowy top high up in the clouds.

We were again asked to dinner in the evening with our friend Napoleon; but our miserly ideas of time have not yet reached the spendthrift East: the minutes sped and no car came to fetch us. With our Western lack of resignation we find it just as hard to wait as the Oriental finds it natural. On one occasion one of my men had arranged to meet someone on the Wednesday at one o'clock; the latter did not come till the day after at twelve noon, and apologized for coming rather late. But Quisling and I could not wait so long as that; when an hour and a half had gone by, we went off on our own account. We dined in a big garden, where the service was at small tables, clean and quite good, and at a moderate price; but there were only a few guests.

The moon rose in the east and smiled down on us through the leafy tree-tops. The dark paths were well fitted for dreaming of the glorious past of this land. A few couples wandered there in the peaceful night, so refreshing after the heat of the day. We were, indeed, in the home of the lovely Georgian women; it was of them that the French jeweller Chardin said 250 years ago: "To see them and not to love them I hold to be impossible." Let us be daring:

Draw back the Chadra! Why dost thou hide thyself?

But perhaps, no! leave the chadra alone, dreams are after all the best there is in life.

Down below us the Kura ripples on its way to the sea through the storied land. We hear the Georgian's sorrowful song:

And once more the old wound throbs,
O land of mine, that once wast so richly gifted,
it is to me as though thy past lay buried
in this stream, whose weeping strikes my ear.[1]

---

[1] By the Georgian poet, Elias Chavchavadse, translated (into Danish) by Alfred Ipsen.

In the garden there was a variety show, with a travelling company from Moscow, but not a seat was to be had. As usual, they acted excellently and won great applause. It is remarkable what a decided gift the Russian people, and I think these Caucasians also, have for scenic representations of every kind: acting, both drama and tragedy, comedy and burlesque, and opera, not to speak of dancing, the ballet, and spectacles. All kinds of performances are highly valued by the whole people. It is worthy of note that, when the Soviet government in Moscow had under consideration the suppression of the famous ballet and opera, since the yearly cost was so heavy, the whole of the working-class population sent in a petition against this measure. This is, so far as I know, the one and only time that the working men have been united on a petition; but they wanted their ballet, and the government did not do away with it.

What is striking is that with all their feeling for scenic display and magnificence they show no inclination this way in their own behaviour or dress. The men, who here are in a great majority, make a monotonous impression in their gray or white blouses with soft gray Lenin caps; nor do the women one sees here show any bright colours; here and there a shawl or blouse in staring colours, but there is no holiday dress, only a gray, colourless, inartistic mass in workaday clothes. But maybe this is how it is to be in the new society; the old days are gone with their luxury, their bright splendour and festivities, with gold and rustling silk, and with their great vices—all at the cost of the workers. Of artistic understanding, of interest in what is going on on the stage, it may be that there is as much to be found in this "proletarian" audience which now fills the seats and boxes as there was in most of the former gold and silk-clad ladies and gentlemen.

While we were thus taken up with watching this crowd, suddenly there stood before us our friend Napoleon. Along with his friends he had been looking for us in all the places of entertainment in Tiflis, until at last he found us here. He had been so busy making preparations for our departure next day that he had been greatly delayed. Now compensation had to be made with Kakhetian wine and music; and a small string orchestra played us a last good-bye to Georgia's capital in the plaintive songs of Georgia.

II

THROUGH THE CAUCASUS

THROUGH THE CAUCASUS

While working to soften the dreadful consequences of the great famine of 1921 and 1922 in Russia, I met in Moscow Samursky, the president of the Daghestan Republic. There was also great distress there, and he besought me earnestly to go and see the conditions and to help. I was hindered from doing so, and could do no more than send some of the most necessary medicine; I had now had a telegram from him and his government sending me a hearty invitatioñ to come to Daghestan on my way home. As there was nothing to hinder me, I wired back that Quisling and I would be in Vladikavkaz on Monday, July 6th.

Instead of taking the long railway journey round the east of the Caucasus, first to Baku and so along the coast of the Caspian Sea through Derbent to Daghestan, we wished to drive by motor-car along the so-called Georgian military road right across the Caucasian range.

We were now told many tales of the many remarkable things that may happen on this road. The year before, the mail-carrier had been shot right beside the passenger, who had been robbed of everything and left stripped to the skin on the road. In the spring a passenger in the post-car had been so unlucky as to get a bullet through both knees, so that he had been left with them stiff ever since. These rugged mountain-folk in the high impassable valleys of the Caucasus, where every man carries arms, find it hard to give up their old ways altogether. But we were told that the road would now be quite safe.

THE CAUCASUS RANGE

The Caucasus range stretches as a sharply marked off, relatively narrow, but high unbroken ridge right across the land between the Caspian and the Black Sea, from Baku in the south-east to the mouth of the Sea of Azov in the north-west. With a length of 1,100 and a breadth of 70–170 kilometres, it covers an area of over 120,000 square kilometres. For a length of 700 kilometres the mountains are over 3,000 metres high; and with its narrow, high, and dangerous passes, 2,300 to over 3,000 metres high, this mountain wall has played a great part in history through shutting off the wanderings of peoples from both south and north, so that in most cases they had to seek a way either east of the Caspian or over the straits to the west of the Black Sea.

The Caucasus has the shape of a mighty vault or fold in the earth's crust, with some lesser folds along the north side. The main fold is thrust up highest in the central part between the sources of the Kuban and the Terek, and is canted over towards the south, with dizzy precipices on this steep southern slope. In this central part the ridge is made up of crystalline, granitic rocks; they may belong to the basic rock itself, which in other parts of the chain is covered by heavy sedimentary layers.

North of this central ridge of basic rocks there broke out at a relatively late time two mighty volcanic masses lying on top of the basic rock: one north-west with the volcano Elbruz or Djin-Padishah (King of the Spirits, 5,629 metres) as its highest peak, and one in the south-east with the volcano Kasbek (5,043 metres). These volcanic masses make up the highest points in the range, and more than twenty of them are higher than Mont-Blanc. They are usually separated from the main ridge and the watershed by lengthwise valleys, and consist in great part of trachytes; but they have also sent forth great streams of basaltic lava down the mountain-sides.

The south-east part of the range, from the stretch by the sources of the Terek, near Kasbek, as far as the Caspian and Baku, is mostly made up of sedimentary layers in consecutive series from the Lias and Jura to the Cretaceous formation and the beginning of the Tertiary. The northern ridge, known as the Andi range, in Daghestan, which runs through Chechnia to the plain west of Petrovsk, seems to be a continuation in a way of the Meshi mountains and the Surnam ridge (with the low watershed between the Rion and Kura valleys), which runs south-west to north-east, and then, on the north side of the main range, east-north-east and east. This adds to the breadth of the mountain-land of Daghestan. The heights of the mountains in this east and south-east part of the Caucasus are lower than in the central part, although here, too, there are peaks over 4,000 metres high.

On the south the Caucasus falls away to the level land in the low valleys of the Kura and Rion, and on the north to the flat steppes of south-east Russia.

The streams up in the mountains generally follow the valleys, running lengthwise, parallel with the line of the main range, but then break through the ridges in deep narrow gorges. The snow-line on the south side of the range lies at 2,900–3,500 metres; on the north side it lies at 3,300–3,900 metres.

Like the Alps, so too the Caucasus has had an Ice Age, and has been covered with far-reaching snow and ice-glaciers, coming far down towards the lowlands. But it is remarkable that the valleys have not in any degree worthy of mention been . scoured and carved out by the glaciers into a U-shape, as we generally find in glacier-swept lands. Nor have the ice-glaciers hollowed out deep lake-basins in the mountain floor, which is, on the other hand, a characteristic of ice-swept lands, as we find in Norway and Sweden. In the Caucasus the valleys are steep-sided, deep, narrow, and V-shaped; and thus the valley bottoms are narrow, and often hardly allow any passage between their steep walls. Often, too, the streams have cut their way down into deep narrow clefts or cañons. There are no lakes, and the streams hurl themselves down the clefts towards the lowland with water that is nearly always muddy, and does not stop on its way to be cleared in any lake. This water, therefore, is usually good for use on cultivated land, and it leaves heavy deposits at the foot of the mountains.

The reason for the peculiar form of the valleys is probably that the slopes on both sides of the range are so steep that the glaciers found little resistance, while the water, together with the frost, has a strong erosive power, which has been greater than the glaciers'. There is, further, the fact that the types of rock are mostly relatively soft and but little capable of resisting frost and water.

Since the Caucasian mountain ridges were slowly formed by the folding and contraction of the earth's crust, they were originally much lower than they are now. But then erosion has gradually cut its deep valleys through the ridges, and carried much of them away. Through this the earth's crust has been lightened, and has correspondingly risen; the peaks and ridges between the valleys, which have not been greatly affected by erosion, have in this way been raised to the great heights at which they now stand.

These districts, moreover, are in a state of unrest, and are often visited by violent earthquakes, as was Leninakan in Northern Armenia a few years ago. Related to this is probably the tale about the bird Simurg, which has its nest on the top of Djin-Padishah (the King of the Spirits, Elbruz), and with one eye sees the past and with the other the future. When it rises in the air the ground shakes from the beating of its wings, the storms howl, the sea grows rough, and all the sleeping powers of the deep wake to life.

There is probably a connection, too, between the rising and falling of the surface of the Caucasian mountains and of the neighbouring districts and the many hot-springs both north and south of the range. There are also many cold mineral springs; and these hot and cold sulphur and iron springs, and alkaline, iodine, and bromine springs, and others, have been known from olden times for their healing powers. There are many places for treatment and baths to be found in their neighbourhood for the cure of many kinds of sickness and weakness. Tradition has it that even Alexander the Great's men benefited by some of them.

Oil (naphtha) is found in several places round about the edges of these remarkable mountains, but especially in the newest geological layers. Best known is the district of Baku on the Caspian Sea, and then southwards beyond the mouth of the Kura. A rich field, where probably as much oil is now extracted, is near Grozny, south of the river Terek, near its tributary the Sunsha and the streams falling into this. In the flat land south of Petrovsk, along the shore of the Caspian, there is also oil, as also at the opposite north-west end of the range, on the north side, near the Taman peninsula on the Sea of Azov. But oil is found also in Georgia, south of the mountains, between the Kura and its tributary the Alazan. In many places, too, combustible gas comes up from the ground, and in early times with its flame it was an object of veneration to fire-worshippers.

Metals have not up till now been found in great quantities in the Caucasus. Gold is found in some of the streams, but hardly in paying quantities, although Strabo long ago remarked that according to what he had been told "the streams were rich in gold, which is washed out by the barbarians by means of pierced hides and skins with the hair on, and in this way has arisen the tale of the Golden Fleece".

There are considerable deposits of silver, zinc, and lead in the Ossetes' country west of Vladikavkaz. There is also some iron and a little copper; but the most important mines beyond all comparison are the manganese mines in Georgia, on the south slope of the mountains west of Kutais. An American company under Harriman got a concession in 1925 for working these mines, which are, perhaps, the most important in the world's market for the production of manganese. It was a great concern, yielding a large yearly royalty; but owing to disagreements it has now been given up, and the working has been taken over again by the Soviet government. West of Kutais there are also coal-mines. Sulphur, of course, is found in Daghestan.

Of rivers there are in particular four large ones, two north and two south of the Caucasus; and possibly they are related with the four rivers which were believed in the Middle Ages to come forth from the mountain in Paradise; but the mountain and rivers were shifted to the North Pole. The Kuban rises by Elbruz, runs out north over the flat land, and then west into the Sea of Azov. The Terek rises on the south side of Kasbek, runs first east, then north in a foaming course through narrow clefts down past Vladikavkaz and over the flat land, and then makes a sharp bend eastwards, falling into the Caspian with a wide delta. On the south-westerly slope of the mountains is the Rion (the Phasis of the Greeks), which runs by Kutais through its flat valley—the old land of the dawn, Kolkhis—out into the Black Sea. It was from it that Jason fetched the Golden Fleece and the Sun king's fair daughter. The fourth river, and the largest, is the Kura, which runs through its flat valley along the south side of the mountains, and through Azerbaidjan into the Caspian Sea. It does not rise in the Caucasus, but in the highlands to the south, near Kars; but it has many tributaries from the north, among which the Aragva, Yora, and Alazan are the biggest.

On the north of the Caucasus the summers usually have a low rainfall and are hot, while the winters are cold and hard. Taken together there is little rain—near the Sea of Azov about 500 metres, yearly; while in the central part of the mountains it may be about twice as much. On the south of the mountains it is heavier, especially towards the Black Sea, where it may reach 2 metres. These south-western slopes of the mountains are therefore clothed with thick sub-tropical forests, while on the north-east side of the range, in Daghestan, there is so little rain that the mountains are wholly treeless. The mountain slopes towards the north, in the centre and north-west of the Caucasus, are on the contrary clothed with dense forests.

In the lower valleys of the Caucasus the forests are usually made up of oaks, elms, beeches, planes, maples, walnuts, sweet-chestnuts, lindens, poplars, and other leafy trees; and among the trees are twined wild vines, smilax, clematis, and other creepers. Higher up we find the evergreen-oak, horse-chestnut, linden, maple, beech, elm, ash, and aspen, and along the streams the alder; higher up again the birch and the fir begin, until the former gets the upper hand. The tree-line is reached at about 2,200 metres, and above that the pastures go up again towards 3,000 metres.

The animal life is quite a rich one. There are bears, wolves, jackals (which break the peace of night with their howling), hyenas, lynxes, wild-cats, leopards, and also an occasional tiger. Among the game there are many wild pigs and deer in the forests, and in the mountains chamois, ibex, and wild goats. Up in the forests, in the high westerly part of the range, there are also herds of the European bison, one of the few places where there are still found some last remains of this wild ox, which together with the kindred aurochs was once spread over the whole of Europe. Among the game-birds may be especially mentioned the pheasant, of which there are many, and whose original home is here near the river Rion, the Phasis of the Greeks, whence the name.

The domestic animals are cows, sheep, goats, horses, asses, buffaloes. Agriculture is primitive, wooden ploughs are still mostly used, drawn by buffaloes or oxen; but even this is only in the low fertile stretches with a plentiful soil; on the small patches of soil on ledges up on the mountain-side it is only the hoe that can be used. The corn grown is maize, wheat, millet, a few oats, rye, and barley. This last is found growing up to about 2,500 metres. Potatoes and tobacco are also cultivated up to 1,800 metres or so.

As we said above, the Caucasus was a very real barrier to the wanderings of the peoples; the waves washed up these steep slopes from north and from south, and broke against them; but in the inaccessible narrow valleys, where defence was easy, fragments of the passing peoples, or of tribes driven back on north and south, were left behind, shut off in a little world of their own. Thus in these mountains there are more differing races gathered together on a small area than at any other spot in the world. All these peoples speak different tongues, which are mostly but little known, and many of which seem to be but little akin to others that are known.

The many tribes or peoples are usually divided according to their language into three main groups: the true Caucasian, the Turkish-Tatar, and the Indo-European peoples. There are also some others, perhaps, whose origin is still more obscure.

The languages of the *true Caucasians* stand in a peculiar isolation, and so far philologists have not been able to show with certainty any link or kinship with other known languages. Possibly some may have likenesses with several of the languages spoken in Asia Minor in olden times. Some likenesses with Baskish and Etruscan have also been suggested. They are divided into the South Caucasian and the

North Caucasian languages. The former are the various Georgian or Kartvelian languages; while the latter consist of the Abkhasian, Cherkessian, Chechen, and the many Lesghian languages, with others.

The *Georgian peoples* dwell along the Kura and Rion valleys, and on the southern slopes of the Caucasus right up to near the watershed in valleys in the highest part of the mountains (Svanetia, south of Elbruz). The *Abkhasians* live on the southern slopes westwards towards the coast of the Black Sea. The *Cherkesses* (Circassians; or Adigheb, as they call themselves) and the *Kabardians* live on the north side of the Caucasus along the Terek north of Vladikavkaz, and farther west towards the Kuban. After having fought heroically against the Russians and being overcome at last in 1864, the greater part of the Cherkesses migrated to Turkish Asia Minor, where some of them formed roving bands of robbers. The various *Chechen* tribes (true Chechens, Ichkerians, Inguchians with their many lesser tribes, Khists, Karabulag, Michiko) mostly dwell in Chechnia and Ichkeria, north-west of the Daghestan mountains, in the valleys of the Argun and its many tributaries, and northwards as far as Grozny and the Terek, and westwards towards Vladikavkaz. The many *Lesghi* tribes, of whom the Avars are among the best known, are found in Daghestan.

Of the *Indo-European peoples* the *Ossetes* are to be especially mentioned; they live along the west side of the upper courses of the Aragva and Terek, and northwards to west of Vladikavkaz. The *Tats* are also an Indo-European people, living along the coast of the Caspian, north of Baku.

Among the Turkish-speaking peoples may be mentioned the *Kumyks*, who live in the Daghestan coast-lands along the Caspian Sea, and to the south past Derbent; north of them are the *Nogais* in the neighbourhood of the Terek delta. Some *Turkish tribes* also, such as the *Taulus* and the *Karachaevs*, are found dwelling half-way up the mountains west of Elbruz and north of Svanetia.

THE FIRST PART OF THE JOURNEY

At four in the morning, Monday, July 6th, we left Tiflis; our friend Napoleon had made all the arrangements, and came with us in the car. Our expectations were high; we had heard so much about this remarkable road through the Caucasus. The Russians had made a start with it as early as 1783-4, when they also founded Vladikavkaz (that is, the Ruler of the Caucasus). After the road had been finished at the beginning of last century, it was rebuilt at a great expense by Prince Barya-tinsky, the conqueror of Shamyl, and was completed in its present form in 1861.

The first stretch went northwards along the Kura. We then drove through the narrow part of the valley, where the great new dam for the power station has been built across the stream. Here 18,000 horse-power are to be developed now, and later on 30,000. High up on the steep mountain on

the other side was the Church of the Cross like
an eagle's eyry. The way the Georgians had of
building churches upon high inaccessible mountain-
tops like this one was certainly remarkable. The
explanation given by the Frenchman Chardin
(in 1672), that it was "to get out of decorating
them or keeping them up, as it was seldom anyone
went up there", seems hardly to be the right one;
rather we have here, perhaps, an expression of the
Persian doctrine that on the lofty, holy mountains
we are nearer to Heaven and the Lord. But most
likely of all the custom stood also in connection with
security: on such mountain-tops it was easier to
defend oneself and the church's sacred vessels
against the attacks of heathen bands that often
made inroads in the land. This church, like most of
the others, had once been surrounded by a high
wall with watch-towers to strengthen the defence.

The way went on along the Kura, which here
makes a sharp bend southwards through a gorge,
after having come from the west-north-west. Then
the road crosses a bridge, and winds back eastwards
along the left bank of the stream past the oldest
capital of Georgia, Mzkhetha, lying on the tongue of
land where the Aragva from the north falls into the
Kura. Here is the venerable cathedral with the
royal tombs. Then we go north again through the
Aragva valley past an old convent and the ruins of
a fortress. Here we are on holy and historical soil,
filled with memories from the oldest times of the
nation, and with remains from Georgia's prehistory,
and we can feel the melancholy that runs through all

the poetry and music of the nation. Georgia, or rather its central part, Kartlia and Kakhetia, is, indeed, one of the oldest kingdoms in the world, with an almost unbroken line of kings through two thousand years down to the beginning of last century, when it united with Russia. Near the convent have been found many old graves with stone coffins from the Bronze Age, belonging to an older long-headed people quite unlike the Georgians or Kartvelians, who came in later and are predominantly short-headed.

The road goes on along by the river, which has a considerable volume of water with waterfalls, rapids, and whirlpools. In a river like this in Norway there would be water-pixies playing on the harp; here there are nymphs, *russalks*, with long red hair and green eyes, who entice men to them and tickle them till they die.

The road was now slowly rising, and turned to the left away from the Aragva valley. The landscape was less barren; there were green fields, and valley-sides clothed in forest among the bare, stern mountains on the east. We were, however, somewhat astonished to pass a small salt tarn, called Bazaletskoye, which reminded us that it was dry here also near the southern slopes of the mountains; the rainfall was small, indeed, compared with the evaporation.

We drove by the town of Dushet, where the *eristav* (viceroy) of the province of Aragva had his residence in former times. He was very powerful, and often waged war with the kings of Georgia.

There are ruins of a fort from that time. Not far away there is an old grove with a church to Saint Kvirik and Saint Avlita. This church lies on top of a 1,000-metre mountain under venerable holy trees. Such holy trees and groves are often found in the Caucasus, and evidently were old sacrificial places in heathen times.

But on we went through fruitful lands; the mountains around became more and more thickly clothed in forests. We drove down into the valley of the White Aragva, past the town of Ananur, with the ruins of the old stronghold on the mountain slope above it. This latter was surrounded by a wall, which also encloses several churches, and it must have commanded the whole valley in the Middle Ages. It was hither that King Heraklius II, Georgia's old broken lion, fled during the final fight against the Persians in 1795, when Tiflis was taken and ravaged by them, but here it was also that this old hero, well over eighty years old, gathered another small army together, and once more defeated the foe and won Tiflis back.

The mountains rose higher round us, the valley grew narrower, with unbroken forest up the sides, and below us was the foaming stream at the bottom of the valley. Suddenly we turned down to the right away from the road, and stopped before an hotel in a well-grown garden with flowers and trees. This was the stopping-place Passanaur, where we were to breakfast. We were now 1,016 metres above the sea.

Here we met Ter Kasarian's wife and two

47

children, together with our Armenian sporting friend from that evening in Tiflis and his wife. They had come by car just before us. Although Quisling and I had never met the ladies before, we were not introduced, and it was only later on that we by chance came to know who they were, and could pay our respects. This is certainly characteristic of the ways of the country, which are so different from ours. Although we had been now so long a time with our friend Ter Kasarian, who had been our host as representing the government throughout our journey in Georgia and Armenia, yet we had never set eyes on his wife, just as we had not been introduced to any of the leading men's ladies. This is undoubtedly owing to somewhat Eastern views on woman—that she does not count outside her own little world, which is the home. It is perhaps something of the same idea as that which prevents our introducing the woman-servants, and often almost the housekeeper, to our guests. It seemed as though the ladies here do not wish for it either; for if a stranger were introduced to them they would withdraw after exchanging a few words, even if there was no difficulty about the language. They seemed not to be used to playing any part, and to have no wish to do so. Yet women have played important parts in the history of these peoples: we have only to think of Saint Hripsime and her nuns in Armenia, of Nino, who brought Christianity to Georgia, and not least of the mighty Queen Tamara. But in the old noble and princely families of Georgia in the days of knighthood there was undoubtedly another standpoint as regards woman, which shows itself today, among other ways, by the man going third class in the train, but letting the ladies of his family go in the first, when the family means are small.

On the open space before the hotel a half-grown bear was walking about fastened by a long chain. It looked quiet, but at the same time it did not seem advisable for a stranger to come too near; if he did, it would often suddenly run spluttering at him as far as the chain would let it, and evidently with no friendly intentions. Possibly this gives a picture of the true feelings of the Caucasian mountain peoples towards us Europeans. They certainly have no reason to love us. It is the Europeans that have conquered them and robbed them of freedom.

Passanaur seemed to be a thriving little town, with its houses surrounded by nice gardens and leafy trees. The post-station was roomy, with a wide square behind it and long houses, with lofts and upper rooms and all kinds of vehicles below. The forest-clad mountains rose steeply at the sides of the valley.

III

THE MOUNTAIN PEOPLES NEAR THE MILITARY ROAD

THE MOUNTAIN PEOPLES NEAR
THE MILITARY ROAD

THE GEORGIAN MOUNTAIN TRIBES: THE KHEVSURS

We had now come to a district full of ethnographical interest. West of the White Aragva valley the land of the remarkable Ossetes stretches westwards and northwards to the upper valleys of Terek and beyond Vladikavkaz. East of the valley dwell Georgian tribes, the Pshavs, and up in the mountain valleys to the north-east the Khevsurs. They still speak old Georgian dialects; but the latter especially, who number about 8,000, must have lived a long time cut off in their mountain gorges. Their name comes from the Georgian *khevi* (= gorge, cleft). They are still following the customs and ways and superstitions of the Middle Ages. They wear helmets, chain-armour, vambraces and greaves of steel, shields and swords, just like the knights of the Crusades. The helmet is a round steel cap over the upper part of the skull, with a steel net hanging down the back and sides of the head and over the forehead, so that only the eyes and the lower part of the face are left free. On festal occasions, and at martial games and tournaments, they appear in full armour, and so, too, when they fear blood revenge, or when a blood feud between two families or between villages is to be settled by a reconciliation. The reason why these tribes cling to the old weapons is evidently because they have always been living

53

amidst feuds, whether between families or between villages, or with the tribes around them. They are quarrelsome fellows, and always go armed when working out of doors too, usually with shield, sword, dagger, and musket.

A curious custom is that the men wear on the right thumb a thick iron ring with heavy spikes on it; it is used for giving blows in a fight, and there is hardly any older man without unsightly scars due to this cause, and in this hideous disfigurement of the face they often surpass even the most damaged German student. The same kind of ring is said to have been in use in the Black Forest and in Upper Bavaria.

Quarrels often arise, and the dagger sits loose; but wounding and maiming have to be atoned for by a scale of fines. The loss of an eye has to be paid for with thirty cows, a wounded head with three to sixteen cows, a maimed leg with twenty-five, and so on. A cow is looked on as equal to ten roubles. The length of a wound is measured with a thread, and on this barley or wheat grains are laid alternately in their length and breadth, and two-thirds of the number needed to cover the thread must be paid by the culprit in cows.

Among the Khevsurs and the Pshavs, as among most of the Caucasian tribes, blood revenge, of course, is a firmly established custom. Murder must be avenged by the murdered man's kindred, through the death of the culprit, or his kindred, or even people from his village; so that a murder may bring two villages into bloody strife. But the murder can also be atoned for through an agreed fine. For a man eighty cows are paid, for a woman sixty. For the murder of his own wife a man has to pay five cows to her clan (the greater family), but the murder does not call for blood revenge. When a murder affair has been settled, a great atonement-feast is held, animals are sacrificed, and there is much drinking of beer and brandy.

When we hear of these people's life of fighting, we are in many ways reminded of what life was among ourselves in olden times, as it is described in the Icelandic sagas of our forefathers. And right down to the latest times the knife has sat loosely in its sheath among many of our own mountain-folk too.

Nominally these Georgian mountain tribes are Christians, possibly since the 12th century; but they are still living in a world of superstition coming down from very early days. Besides the Christian divinities—God the Father in the seventh heaven, Lord of the heavenly powers and the living; Christ, Lord of the dead; Mary; Peter and Paul, who are the angels of plenty; and others— worship is also paid to many gods of nature. They have a supreme lord over the earth and dry land; there are forest, water, and air spirits in the shape of pigs, lizards, or children. With hunting, two divinities or angels are connected, a man and a woman; the latter is held to be more powerful, and to her are offered the heart, lungs, and liver of the slain beast. Among some tribes she shows herself at times in the forest as a beautiful naked woman with long hair; and to the hunter especially who is brave enough to lie with her she gives good luck, if he holds his tongue, but if he does not, then he has to feel her anger. There are many other protecting spirits; the Khevsurs have also a winged spirit who helps robbers, and whose reward is a share in the booty. Hell is a river of tar, into which poor sinful souls fall from a bridge of a hair's breadth, which they must walk over if they are to reach Heaven; and in this tar they have to swim for all time. Mankind is inventive when it has to describe Hell and Purgatory; we are not so sure what Paradise is like. This bridge, indeed, and the tar river are something like the magic bridge and shifting bogs that had to be crossed by souls in Norway on their way to Heaven in olden times. The bridge as narrow as a thread and the journey of the soul are found among many peoples; among the Arabs it is "narrower than a hair, sharper than a sword, and darker than night".

In one respect the Khevsurs are very pious: they have three holy days of rest in the week: the Mohammedan Friday, the Jewish Saturday, and the Christian Sunday—probably so as to be sure of not offending either Allah, or Jehovah, or the Lord.

These mountaineers live in villages which, like the *a-ul* in Daghestan, are built in terraces up the steep mountain-sides, one house above the other, and so near that the flat roof of one often makes a terrace or a yard before the one above, and the whole, seen at a distance, almost reminds one of the cells in a beehive. The houses are square with a flat roof, generally built of stone and with two floors: the lower for the cattle and women, the upper one for men. It is indeed dirty in these smoky rooms. On the ledges up the steep mountain-sides there is not much cultivation to speak of; generally nothing is done beyond hoeing up the small scattered patches of earth, and growing a little rye, barley, millet, and potatoes. There is but little grass, and they cannot have many cows, sheep, or goats. Generally the living is poor, there is much want. In former days things were better, as they could eke out a livelihood very well with robbery.

They bake bannocks somewhat as we do in Norway, of coarse-ground barley or rye on thin plates over an open fire, generally outside on the ground. These bannocks with sour milk and cheese are the general food. Another likeness with us is that they do not eat fowls or eggs or hares; older Norwegian peasants used not to eat anything with feathers or claws. That the Khevsurs will not eat pork may be owing to Mohammedan or Jewish influences.

Women among these mountain tribes hold a lower position than they would seem to have held among us; they are not much more than chattels and serfs. A man must usually seek his wife in another village, and the old custom says she shall whenever possible be carried off; it is as among so many peoples where the woman was booty in war, to be robbed from other tribes or peoples, while we generally wed within our own stock, or anyhow

within our neighbourhood. The Khevsur bride-
groom comes fully armed with his men-friends
by night to the "women's house" before the village,
where the girl is waiting by arrangement. She has
to show her good bringing up by making a strong
resistance,[1] but he takes her away to his father's
house. After various formalities, whose meaning
would seem to be that they must not show too much
eagerness towards one another, at the end of five
or six days they are married. They are now together
for three nights, but then she goes back again to
her parents for a time before regular married life
begins. If the man is not pleased with his wife, he
can send her back to her parents, and she can
marry again. She also can leave him, but then she
has to buy her freedom, and the amount is so high
that in most cases she cannot manage it. Unfaithful
wives formerly used to have their cheeks slit, or the
nose and ears cut off; but we are not told what was
done to faithless husbands. In former times polygyny
was general, but it is said to be rare now.

A curious belief is that a woman with child is
unclean, and when bringing forth she must stay
alone in a hut outside the village, or anyhow
outside the house. If the birth-throes are difficult,
the only help she gets from the attentive husband is
that he goes stealthily, usually by night, near the
hut, and fires off his gun to frighten the evil spirits
away. After the birth coarse food is brought her by
small girls; but like the mother the vessels she

Among primitive peoples also, like the Eskimos, we find the same
custom, and the same view of good breeding in the woman.

eats from are also unclean, and must not be used by others. She must now stay in the "women's house" (or "cleansing house") outside the village for thirty to forty days before she is once more clean. Women, too, at their periods must betake themselves to it.

Owing to the hard conditions of life they have no wish for many children, and abortion is said to be a general practice. It is not seemly to have a child before the fourth year of wedlock, the second one may come three years later, and three children are enough; but girls are not welcome, although they are not killed, as happened formerly among some tribes.

They make their clothing of wool, torn, and not clipped, from the sheep. It is characteristic that the underclothing is much coarser and heavier than the men's, for whom the finest and softest wool is used.

THE OSSETES

The Ossetes are a people about 225,000 in number, dwelling in Ossetia, on the west of our road to the north. About them there has been much dispute and much written by the learned. They are generally held to be the descendants of the Indo-European Alans, and perhaps partly, too, of the Massagetians mentioned by Herodotus; they have also been connected with his Sarmatians. Ptolemaeus (2nd century A.D.) called them Ossilians, while for the Arab and medieval writers they are Assans or Alans. In the Russian chronicles in the beginning of the

12th century they were known as Yasses or Yossi. They call themselves Ironians, which has been held to be the same as Aryon, which again is the same as the name Alan; but by others Ironians has been held to be exactly the same word as Iranians. Their tongue is Indo-European, belonging to the Iranian branch, and wholly different from both the North Caucasian and the South Caucasian languages.

They must have come to the Caucasus from the north, and in the 1st century of our era they were widely spread throughout Southern Russia, where they dwelt along the lower Don. This name is the Ossetian word for water; we find it, too, in many names of streams on the north side of the Caucasus, such as Ar-don (= headlong water) and others. The Sea of Azov, along whose east side the Ossetes dwelt, has probably also got its name from them.

At the beginning of the wanderings of the peoples a great part of the Alans or Ossetes with the Goths and Huns went westwards, and settled on the Danube, whose name may come from them. They may have founded, too, the town of Jassy (pronounced Yash) in Moldavia. From the 7th to 13th centuries first the Khazars and then the Mongols drove back the Ossetes from the Don district southwards to the rivers Kuban and Terek. They were originally a powerful nation of horsemen, but finally, in the 14th century, the Kabardians coming in from the Crimea drove them up into the mountains to the district they now dwell in. That in early times they knew the mountains and were settled near them is perhaps pointed to by the fact that their word *khokh* (= mountain) would seem to be the first letters in the Greek name (Καύκασος).

Compared with the other peoples, especially the eastern Caucasians, the Ossetes are fairly long-headed (the mean index is perhaps about 81). Their eyes are mostly blue or gray, their hair and beard generally blond, light-brown, or reddish. The face is often broad, the nose big and straight, the lips thin, the face is fair, often ruddy. On the whole they are of middle height and sturdy build, both men and women. Originally the Ossetes may have been partly of Nordic race, or there has been a strong immigrant element from the north, while their speech points to a predominating part of them having had eastern connections with the Iranian peoples. The variations in the shape of the head, and the blending with dark hair and brown eyes, may point to a strong mixture with tribes in their neighbourhood in later times.

For us Northerners this people has a certain interest in that their name has been set in connection with the Old Norse name *áss* for our gods. Snorre Sturlason tells us in the Ynglinga saga that the land east of the river Tanakvisl (Tanais = Don) in Asia was called Åsaland or Åsaheim, but the capital of the land was called Åsgard, and there Odin was the ruler. Although Snorre would connect Åss with the name Asia, yet we may well think of the Ossetes, who indeed dwell east of the Tanakvisl or Don; Åsaland then becomes the land of the Ossetes. It is noteworthy that Snorre also tells us that Odin had great possessions south of the "great mountain-belt", that is, the Caucasus (just where some of the Ossetes now dwell), and that "at that time the Roman Emperors went far abroad in the world, and brought all the peoples under themselves". The far-sighted Odin then went away, "and all his gods with him and many other peoples", first westwards to Gardarike (= Russia), then southwards to Saksland (= Germany), and then northwards.

Philologists derive the word *ass* or *áss*, Old Germanic *ans—ansu*, from the root *ans* = "to breathe" or "blow"; so that *áss* would then more or less mean a wind-god, or a spirit. But this would not prevent the name being in some way or other related later with the Ossetes, who also may have had an *a*-sound in their name (compare the Sea of Azov).

Most of the Ossetes are now nominally Christians —Orthodox Greeks—and about a fourth of them are Mohammedans; but like the Khevsurs they are all still more or less heathen, and worship their old gods and spirits. That some of these have been given saints' names has hardly made them less heathen. Thus the god of thunder and lightning is called Saint Elias, but seems to have a likeness with our thunder god Thor. When anyone is killed by lightning, he has been struck by Saint Elias for having offended him. The dead man is buried either where he was killed or on the spot the body happens to be drawn to when it has been laid on a two-wheeled cart harnessed to two rams. At the grave a black ram is slaughtered, and the skin is hung up on a pole. These two rams that decide where the body is to be buried may be looked on as the rams of Elias, the thunder god; and may it not be that they and the two-wheeled cart have some connection with the car of the god Thor? The holy Elias also saves mankind from Ruimon, the blind-born dragon that dwells in the world beyond, and by its roaring brings sickness and death on men. He fastens a chain to it, and drags it up to the plains above, where the spirits of Heaven cut lumps of flesh from it, which the souls cook and eat, and so are made young. This seems to have a likeness to Thor and the World-snake, which lay outside the world, and which in Jotunheim he hooked and dragged up to the plain above.

The Ossetes have also many gods watching over the various activities of life: there is the supreme god of good and evil, who must always be called upon; then there is the god that sentences to death on the way from Paradise to Hell; the sun's son; the moon's son; gods of the fields, the harvest, cattle, game, the waters, fishes, health; a god who watches over robbers, and many others. To the god of evil the father of the household slaughters a lamb before his door on the Wednesday evening between Christmas and the New Year. This god is given food and drink and is prayed to that he may do no evil to the house or the cattle. A feast is held by night, but the name of the supreme god must not be utered during the whole entertainment. This is as it is with us: if a man wants to get friends with the Devil, God's name must not be uttered, for then he at once disappears.

Of great importance are the spirits (*safa*) of forefathers, and the household spirit, the warden of the hearth, who must be treated with special consideration. For him a ram is slain at stated times, the blood being buried in the ground; and for him food is also set out from time to time, or for the dead, often at certain spots in the forest. These are ideas from the oldest times, even before heathendom, and are found among many peoples. They are very like our own ideas about the good-man (*hauge-bonne*), and to some extent the brownie. The former is really the family's founder, or the general idea of all the dead forefathers, and for him good food and Yuletide ale are set out under some tree sacred to him; and drink may also be poured out for him on the hearth.

Among the Ossetes as among the Georgian mountain tribes—the Khevsurs, Pshavs, Tushes, Shvans (Svanetians), and others—it is in holy groves that the tribes gather for the worship of God and at sacred festivals. These groves consist of various kinds of leafy trees, and are usually found in spots which otherwise are clear of forest. They are evidently often old heathen places of sacrifice, and in them the tribes have their holy places—altar and churches. At the festivals animals are sacrificed and the blood is smeared on the altar and on the people; beer is brewed, and great quantities of it are drunk, together with spirits, while the sacrificial animals are eaten. Women are forbidden, even at the festivals, to go into these groves, or to touch the holy trees. In some places there are groups of

NORTH OF GUDA-UR

BOYS AT GUDA-UR POST-STATION

ALONG THE VALLEY PAST KOBI

holy trees where weddings, too, are held. In a sacred grove only the priests belonging to it can take part in brewing the beer. If anyone else dares to fell a tree there, or even break off a twig, the god of the place strikes him with a serious illness or death. In a holy grove by Abanokan in the Trusso gorge it is Saint Ilya (Elias) who strikes the evil-doer with blindness, and to get his sight back again he must sacrifice an ox.[1]

Holy trees and groves are found among many peoples; we have also had them in the north (cp. Upsala). At Börte (Mo, Telemark) there was a grove that was held so sacred that not even the grass there could be cut or grazed, as otherwise someone would have a misfortune.[2]

A curious circumstance is that under certain trees in the sacred groves of the Ossetes great heaps of twigs can be seen: anyone passing by a sacred grove of this kind is bound to put a twig or a bit of wood there as an offering to the god of the place. In Norway there are many places where the same custom is followed, and the same great heaps of twigs may be seen by paths in the forest, where passers-by leave a twig according to an old custom, whose reason no one knows. In some places small stones are left in the same way as offerings.

In olden times unhewn stones some three metres high were often set up on Ossete graves; they may be something of the same kind as our own *bauta* stones.

[1] C. Hahn, *Kaukasische Reisen und Studien*, Leipzig, 1896, pp. 124 f.; and *Aus dem Kaukasus*, Leipzig, 1892, p. 63.
[2] Cp. Moltke Moe, in Amund Helland, *Norges Land og Folk*, VIII, Bratsberg Amt, vol. i, pp. 415 ff., Kristiania, 1900.

The Ossetes have an enviably practical way of getting their rights. When a man cannot get what he is entitled to from another, or cannot get a wrong righted, he threatens to kill a dog or a cat on the grave of the other man's forefathers, whose souls in the other world are then threatened with the shame of being tormented by these beasts. The thought of this no Ossete can bear, and the matter is at once settled. When an Ossete takes an oath he holds a dog by the tail, or an ass by the ear; then if he swears falsely the souls of his forefathers or kinsmen will have to eat the same kind of beasts in the world beyond. The same conceptions are also found among the Khevsurs, and most probably are connected with an old worship of forefathers.

The Ossete villages up here in the mountains are not big—from twenty or thirty houses down to five or six, lying on terraces up the steep mountainsides. Higher up the houses may lie scattered, each by itself, but then they are like fortified strongholds. The houses in the mountain valleys are of stone, like those of the Khevsurs; lower down they are also built of wood with bond-work like the Norwegian wooden house. There are always high towers for defence in the villages, and in many places one for every house. These quarrelsome people have to be always ready to defend themselves. It is significant, too, that among them theft or robbery from those of another tribe is not looked on as a crime; it is as though they are always at war.

Each village makes up a commune with an "elder" as its head; this again is divided into "great families" with a father of the household for each one; but this great family no longer seems to be closely united, and the property is not held in common. When a man dies his property is divided in equal shares among the sons, but the eldest gets the house and some cattle over and above his share, and the youngest some cattle and weapons. The daughters get nothing; on the other hand, on marriage a sum is paid for them, which goes to the father or the brothers, they being, more or less, property that can be sold. Among most of the Ossete tribes there are no distinctions of rank or class.

The Ossetes live by husbandry, but still more by cattle-raising, especially up in the mountains; in former times robbery was also quite an important way of livelihood. In the lower valleys there is sometimes a rotation of crops: in the first year on the newly manured land wheat or maize is raised, in the second year barley, and in the third year it is left fallow. Oats and millet are also grown, and peas, beans, potatoes, cucumbers, and so on. In the upper valleys it is usually rye and barley that are grown; but up on the mountain slopes there are no very big patches of earth, and cattle-raising is the main thing. They have sheep mostly, and some goats, cows, and horses. The cattle in the summer spend the night in a field near the house, fenced round with a stone wall or hurdles like our own cattle; on winter nights they are in byres, generally on the lower floor of the dwelling-house, as among the Khevsurs. The dung is collected and mostly put on the fields. But this is not the custom among other Caucasian peoples; like the Russians they use the dried cow-dung for fuel, of which up in the bare treeless mountains there is very little. The dung is kneaded into cakes, and often piled up against the house walls to dry in the sun.

In the forested valleys the forests are also worked to some extent, and the timber is floated as in Norway. The streams are swift-flowing and full of obstructions, and the timber often gets held up and has to be cleared.

The men do the heavy outdoor work: ploughing, haymaking, thrashing, wood-cutting, rafting, carpentry, masons' work, etc. The women work in the house, milk and drive the cows and small cattle, spin and weave; they also work in the fields, cut the corn with sickles, bring brushwood from the forest, and so on.

The death of a man, needless to say, is a great event in these small societies, and among the Ossetes and Khevsurs is celebrated with great ceremony, in which the whole village takes part with mourners and wailing women, and horse-races, much feasting, beer, and spirits. The burial and the journey to the land of the dead are bound up with old heathen customs. In the year following up to twelve memorial festivals are held, to which the people of the neighbouring villages are bidden. This has to be done so that the dead man in the other world may get the sacred bread, beer, and spirits, and not have to eat grass. But the widow has to fast a whole year, and wear a coarse black shift and skirt, while every Friday she must go to the grave with food and drink for the dead man.

This people's wooden vessels and cooking and household gear seem to be like those of the old Germans in many ways, as also their custom of brewing beer from barley. This last is also a Khevsur custom, but other Caucasian tribes usually brew a kind of millet-beer.

The fact that many of the Ossete ways and customs, and many of their implements, have great likenesses with those to be found among us northern Germans is probably in part owing to a common Indo-European origin; but, of course, it may also be a result of a sameness of life and its conditions. It is to be noted that many like customs are found not only among their neighbours, the Khevsurs and Pshavs, but also among other tribes of quite different origin and speech.

IV

OVER THE CAUCASUS

OVER THE CAUCASUS

At Passanaur the White Aragva, coming from the north and north-west, joins the Black Aragva, coming from the mountains in the north-east. The names for the colours of these streams are due to the mud carried down by them, which again varies with the nature of the ground. If the rocks are hard, the water is clear, and the stream gets a dark look from its bed and its depth, and is called black or dark; if the rocks are softer the water carries mud along with it of the colour of the rocks.

We drove north and north-west along the left bank of the White Aragva, which came foaming down towards us at the bottom of the green forest-clad valley. The villages are still mainly Georgian, but also partly Ossete on the west side of the valley, which latter strikes one at once as being poorer.

We drove on steadily at a good speed up along the valley, the road steadily rising. High up on the steep slopes on the west side of the valley hung Ossete villages with old defence towers. It is so steep up there that hay and crops must be carried on the back or in sleds. When villages were built on such inaccessible spots it was mainly for defence; fortified as they were with towers, they were not easy to take. The conditions were hard: there was always fighting, always defence against attacks and robbery, always heavy toil besides—such was the life of these mountain tribes.

East of the valley towards the land of the Khevsurs there are no villages to see; they keep farther away from the outside world and in their mountain gorges.

When the village of Mleti (1,513 metres above the sea) has been passed—it lies on a high precipice over the Aragva—the road crosses a bridge over the foaming waters, and here the mountain world starts in earnest. Up to now the road has been able to follow the gradually rising valley along the stream; but now there is an end to this, and we cannot help asking ourselves whether we are really to climb those high precipitous mountain walls that soar before us. But yonder winds the road, indeed, bend after bend, till it disappears high up over the rim.

Up, up we went, turn after turn, forwards and backwards, higher and higher. The valley sank deeper and deeper at every bend; we could not see the precipice below us, but only knew that the edge of the road fell sheer down hundreds of metres. Some of the bends were so sudden that we had to take the car to the very edge of the precipice so as to swing round.

As we climbed higher and higher we had a wide view up and down the valley. We saw the Aragva like a white ribbon of foam deep down in the abyss, and the villages clinging like swallows' nests to the mountain walls below us on the other side, with patches of field and green grass let into the steep slopes around them. Behind this again the view opened as far as the snowy mountains; peak rose behind peak—the Red Mountain and then the Seven Brothers, which are made up of reddish volcanic rocks. There were snow and glaciers everywhere, and in between were deep clefts and ravines with perpendicular sides, and white foaming streams at the bottom. At last we came to the edge of the abyss; and now to our left we could look right down into Gud-khevi, the Devils' Gorge, through which the Aragva plunges as it comes out from the mountains—a dizzy narrow abyss, deep down between almost perpendicular walls in the lofty mountains. It was all like some mighty giant aroused and turned to stone in his fury.

Soon we reached Guda-ur, at 2,160 metres above the sea, the highest post-station on the whole road. Here and there is a meteorological station also. The road rose along the east side of the Aragva gorge, skirting the dizzy precipices. The scenery grew wilder and wilder. In many places the road was covered by a roof on pillars against snow and stone avalanches. We often drove by children, who were probably looking after the cattle that were browsing along the grass-clad mountain-side. They danced about in front of the car on the very edge of the precipice, and threw small bunches of flowers into it as a greeting or welcome to us, after the custom of the land, but they did not beg.

Then we came to the highest part of the Krestovi pass (that is, the Cross pass), about 2,380 metres above the sea; it is marked by a stone pillar, and opposite it on the right side of the road there stands an old cross, from which the pass is probably named; it is said to have been set up there by Queen Tamara. Up here in the mountains, too, her name still lives. In many places there are small old stone churches, or the ruins of them, and tradition says they were built by her. It is said that she herself at the head of the warriors penetrated into the high mountain valleys, subdued the savage mountain tribes, and brought them Christianity. This still lives in song on the people's lips in Svanetia:

> . . . and the mountains bowed before her.
> Tamar came to Svan-land, wearing her crown.
>
> Tamar's eyes were like precious stones.
> Over her silk kirtle she wore a coat of mail.
> Tamar had a belt of gold;
> Tamar wore her royal sword at her side.

It is quite likely that this remarkable woman, mild yet strong, did reach the high mountain valleys in her expeditions.

We were now standing on the watershed between the basin of the Kura to the south and that of the Terek to the north. We said good-bye to Georgia's lovely valleys with all their memories, to its people that for two thousand years has fought for its freedom and culture, and to that soil soaked with the blood of its noblest sons. But the sons of Georgia still sing:

> Thou art not yet dead, home of my fathers,
> thou dost but sleep, awaiting the morrow;
> then shalt thou deck them with the victor's wreath,
> who for thy sake have kept their watch among the dead.[1]

---

[1] From the Georgian poet, Akaki Zereteli, translated (into Danish) by Alfred Ipsen.

Fair kingdoms, indeed, there have been in the world! How much that was lovely and full of life have we men not laid waste and destroyed in fighting and warfare—and to what end?

As we went on we came to a still wilder and more forbidding landscape, with gray mountain-sides, scraped utterly bare. The road sloped slightly downwards, and the streams ran north. We came down into a narrow cleft along a stream that runs foaming down to the great Terek. This is a dangerous stretch owing to avalanches in the winter and spring, as the long galleries bear witness. We stopped at a spring rich in carbonic acid that gushed out from the rock, and had to drink health and strength from its refreshing waters. Several boys and men gathered round the car and offered rock-crystals and other minerals for sale.

We had, as I said, now left the crest of the mountain chain and the watershed behind us, and were steadily coming lower; but before us we had the mighty volcanic masses that have broken up through the basic rock on the northern slope of the mountain fold, and tower up as great volcanoes, of which Kasbek is the highest. Now and then we caught a glimpse of the giant Mkin-vari's proud snowy peak through the sea of clouds.

The land northwards from here is mostly inhabited by Ossetes. Near the station of Kobi we came upon the Terek in the valley on the south of the Kasbek group; it flows headlong from west-north-west out of the gloomy Trusso gorge between sheer cliffs.

We followed the right bank of the river. At Kobi there rose defiantly a lofty, dark wall of basalt with its six-sided columns. The valley now widened, but its sides were steep and bare. On ledges up them were perched small, generally Ossete, villages with their square defence towers telling of the constant fighting of these people, even in this barren landscape; here, too, are tribal feuds, the never-ending blood revenge between families, and robbery.

On a dominating hill in the valley was the old fortress of Sion. In this valley there is a birch-grove which has been watched over from olden times by the Ossete peasantry, being held sacred by them. It lies about 1,800 metres above the sea.

At length we reached the well-known station of Kasbek, which has a big hotel. The road had now come down to 1,715 metres above the sea, or about 600 metres below the watershed. On the west side of the valley stood a high rock with buildings, most probably a church, on top; but behind it everything was hidden in the swirling mists, and one could but dimly feel the presence of a wonder-world.

But as we gazed up there, suddenly there was a rift high up in the curtain, and amid the whirling masses of cloud there hung a mighty white glacier over us from the sky. One caught one's breath; it seemed to be beyond belief; but the highest peak stood dizzily clear for a moment, and then once more the dreamlike sight was hidden again in the clouds.

It was Kasbek (Mkin-vari), 5,043 metres high, over 3,300 metres above where we stood. It was up there that Zeus chained Prometheus, who, having stolen fire from Heaven and given it to mankind, thought he could also defy the unswerving laws of the gods, and in open fight with the mighty ones snatch power and happiness for the children of men. Up there above the dizzy cliffs the foolhardy dreamer chafes in his chains, whilst the greedy vulture of envy gnaws at his liver. It is the old tale of our erring kind, which seeks to storm Heaven and steal happiness, but is left hanging on the edge of the abyss; it is the spirit of Cain, the rebel, with the hot greed that knows no bounds.

According to what is told by some of the mountain-dwellers the hero is now old, his hair is white like his beard, which reaches to his feet, and his whole body is covered with white hair. Around his body and hands and feet are iron chains fastened to the rock. Only a few men can gaze upon him, since it is so dangerous to climb the high, steep mountains and snowfields, and none can look at him twice; those that have tried have never come back. There are some old people in the mountains that have spoken with him. They may not tell of all they have seen and heard. But the old man is sore glad and rejoiced when he can see people. There are three things he asks about: whether strangers yet ride through the land, and towns and villages are built; whether the young folk in all the land are yet being taught in schools; and whether the wild fruit-trees bear much fruit. If, as is usual, the answer is No, he is greatly afflicted.

The first of ordinary mortals to climb Kasbek was the well-known English mountaineer Freshfield; together with Moore, Tucker, and the Chamonix guide François Devouassoud he reached the top in 1868. It is the highest mountain in this part of the Caucasus; but far away to the west-north-west is another mighty volcanic mass, which likewise has broken out on the northern slope of the range, and which has still higher volcanoes —the highest being Elbruz, 5,629 metres above the sea.

The fact of both volcanic masses lying separated from the main range gives these volcanoes a still more overwhelming effect, and makes them so clearly visible far off and from may sides.

In the village of Kasbek and in the larger one of Gergeti, opposite it on the other side of the stream, Georgian mountaineers live; while in the a-ul of Gveleti, 7 kilometres farther north, there are mostly Chechens, who have been noted ibex-hunters. The Chechens' land is on the east side of the Terek valley north of the Khevsurs; otherwise to the north the valley right down to the flat land is inhabited by Ossetes.

Near Kasbek an old graveyard has been found, which is held to belong to the Bronze Age. Already at that time, therefore, there were men living here in the upper Terek valley, and there must have been traffic through the narrow pass. As in many places about the Caucasus, various objects from Bronze Age culture have been found, among others phallic figures, pointing to a phallic cult.

TYPES AT THE MINERAL SPRING

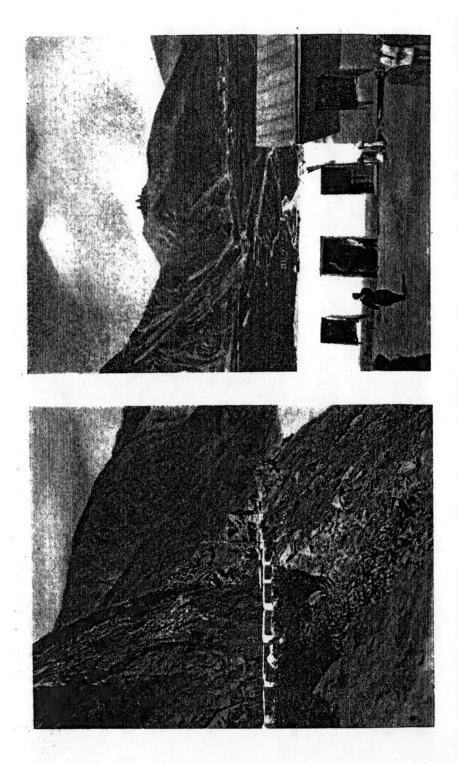

Here, too, amidst this mighty landscape men have worshipped the life-force and fruitfulness.

The road led along the foaming Terek, which bears with it a whitish mud, probably holding lime or clay. From here there is another glimpse up the Devorak valley towards the glacier that takes its rise from the snowfields of Kasbek. This was the glacier which last century brought such heavy disaster, for it spread far down and held up a stream, until the dammed up waters broke through the ice and brought destruction down the whole of the Terek valley.

We drove over a bridge to the left side of the valley. The valley narrowed; the rocky walls rose sheer on both sides for 1,000–1,500 metres straight up from the stream, which whirled along far below us. The Terek now cuts its deep gorge towards the north, right through the high ridge in front. There was hardly room for the road, and often it was cut into the perpendicular or even overhanging wall, with a hundred metres sheer fall into the whirling stream. The mountains hereabouts were high, and mostly too steep for any trees to grow; and few patches of grass were to be seen on the ledges. The rocks were of a soft kind, and there were many fresh marks of landslides and avalanches.

The road wound down the mountain-side through the wild ravines, while the telegraph and telephone wires stretched from pole to pole, or hung on the mountain wall and spanned the clefts. Unceasingly these thin wires carry silent messages through this isolated mountain world from one community to another—it may be the latest gossip, or it may be a message deciding men's fate.

We were in the Darial Gap (that is, the Gate of the Alans; Persian, *dar-i-Alan*), also known as the Gate of the Iberians (or of the Sarmatians). How, one may well ask, can there have been any passage here for men and livestock and caravans, not to speak of great armies and whole peoples with their baggage, before this road was made? But we also know that people went through here already in the Bronze Age, 4,000 years ago, and probably long, long before then. Through here in the 8th century B.C. the Kimmerian bands marched, and fell on Georgia and the kingdom of the Khaldians in what is now Armenia, threatening Assyria. From Strabo's description (xi, 3, 5) of the crossing over the mountains (which took seven days), we may also conclude that there was a regular road in his time, about the beginning of our era. The Arab Yakut-el-Hamavi (about A.D. 1230) speaks of the pass as being the way to the Alans' land, and he mentions, moreover, a bridge over the stream (see below). In 1769 the Russian general Todleben with four hundred men and four guns went through the pass to Tiflis, and in 1783 the Russians took four guns this way; next year they began building a military road to it from the north. The present splendid road was completed, as we said above, in 1861.

In olden times also there must have been some kind of road partly built by the hand of man through this narrow gap; anyhow, something must have been done to make things easier at the worst places, where the rock walls fall straight down into the swirling stream. It is quite possible that when at certain seasons the stream was low, there was some kind of passable road along the bed of the stream. But when it is swollen, as it was now, the rushing waters fill the whole bottom of the gorge, and there is no way through it to be seen for men or wingless cattle along the perpendicular sides. It must have always been easy for a small force to shut this gateway against the strongest army.

We came down again to the stream, and a bridge led over to the right side. But the gap grew still narrower; it was as if we were squeezed into the very floor of this rent in the mountains, between the mighty, lofty masses of rock. It is only nigh to Hell that there can be such a road. Farther on the way was quite shut to us; there could not be any passage. But the way down must be here. And when we came nearer, a narrow cleft opened where the stream raced through.

This was evidently the gate itself, and before it on the left side of the river was a little Russian fort with round, strong towers at the corners, flat on top, with breastwork sand embrasures for guns, and loopholes in the walls.

According to old Georgian writers, King Mirvan of Mzkhetha in the 3rd century B.C. shut this gap with a wall and strong iron gates, and there are said to be remains of the wall. Strabo (about the beginning of our era) says that "a fortress wall difficult to take guards the end of the road". Pliny

(1st century A.D.) says of "the Caucasian Pass, which many wrongly call the Caspian Pass," that "here there are gates with iron-studded beams; under them runs an evil-smelling stream, and up on the mountain on this side of the pass lies a strong fortress called Cumania, which has barred the way for countless peoples. At this spot, which lies right opposite the Iberic town of Harmastes, the land is thus shut off with gates." Possibly there is here a confusion with the fortifications at Derbent, east of the Caucasus on the Caspian. The evil-smelling stream may, on one supposition, have reference to the naphtha springs and gas rising out of the ground there. The Arab geographer Yakut-el-Hamavi (about A.D. 1230) tells us that "in the Caucasian Pass, whereby the Alans are reached, lies the stronghold of Bab-Allan (the Alans' Gate), a most remarkable place; there a very few men can bar the way over the mountain. It lies impregnable on a steep rock and has a spring. Before the stronghold there is a deep valley, across which a bridge leads that is right under the castle wall, and is fully commanded by it."

But however that may have been, it seems almost an impossibility for even a great army, without the artillery of today, to have got through here, so long as the place was held by a handful of brave and stout warriors of the kind reared by these mountain tribes.

On a high hill behind the Russian fort were the ruins of an old Ossete stronghold. This was Tamara's. So, as we took leave of this land of wonders, this magic name rang in our ears as a last greeting. That the fortress was built by her is not very likely, but undoubtedly the fair queen's strong arm reached as far as this over the mountain rampart, and her little well-shaped hand held the key to the gate shutting the wild Darial gap and the entrance to her kingdom.

Before we reached the station farther on with the name (which sounded so homelike) of Lars, a bridge again took us over the stream to the left side. In the narrow valley one saw watch-towers here and there on jutting points of the mountain. Then, as it widened out, the mountains grew lower, and the slopes were clad with forest. Up on the right hand was a fort. The mountains drew farther and farther back, and the road went along between forest-clad spurs.

The view now opened out on to the plain before us; there lay the town of Vladikavkaz ("The ruler of the Caucasus"), and we whirled along over the broad green flats smiling in the sunshine. The deep, gloomy gorge that had brought us through the mighty mountains was now behind us.

We reached the town about midday, having spent eight hours on one of the most remarkable drives anywhere—hours filled with an unbroken succession of new, and ever more overwhelming, impressions, so that the mind could barely take them in. It was the same journey for which a traveller in the 'thirties of last century had to spend a whole month.[1] The restlessness of European

---

[1] Cp. C. F. Lehmann-Haupt, *Armenien Einst und Jetzt*, 1910, vol. i, p. 53.

THROUGH THE CAUCASUS TO THE VOLGA

civilization had driven us onwards, and prevented us from travelling slowly and stopping to take in at our leisure all the manifold wonders we had gone through. We see and experience much, but it is on the surface only; we never get time to make it our own and deepen our knowledge. It was with a sharp feeling of how fleeting all is today that we drove across the bridge over the Terek, and then up the broad main street of Vladikavkaz with rows of lindens on each side.

It was some festival day or other, and there were processions and demonstrations in the streets, with great masses of people and speeches. We were met by two envoys from Daghestan wearing the handsome Caucasian dress, with the stiff coat (*cherkeska*) —one in black, the other in gray, upright and slender-waisted—and with belts carrying the beautifully worked daggers, broad strips of cartridges on their chests, and the becoming lambskin cap. They looked very splendid, and were to bring us to Daghestan, the train leaving in the afternoon. Meanwhile we were hospitably entertained in a charming gentleman's house.

Vladikavkaz lies about 700 metres above the sea on both sides of the Terek, in the wide plain that runs north from the foot of the mountains. The town was founded in 1784 at the starting-point of the military road over the Caucasus, which the Russians began building at that time. These many good roads, which have been built by Russia in so many places for overcoming and holding other peoples under with her armies, have served a good purpose, too, by opening the way to peaceful men.

The town became the fortified capital of the Terek province, and the central base for the relentless advance from the north on the Caucasian peoples. Its main value, therefore, has been as a garrison town, and it has no antiquities of interest. We walked a bit through the streets, which are laid out with that extraordinary width usual in Russia, where there is so much room to spare. We went by the former governor's palace; it looked forlorn, and on the wide square before it grass was growing between the flags; instead of parades and stiff soldiers and officers, and governors with fluttering cocked-hats, the only sign of life now was a big pig rooting and grunting, and philosophizing on this world's ups and downs, together with a flock of geese. *Sic transit* . . . But it may be that these new-comers are just as useful.

We visited the museum, whose director received us most kindly and showed us round. Its ethnographical collections from the many Caucasian peoples were especially interesting to us. Among other things we saw here many of the Ossete implements and utensils. From the roof we had a wide view over the trees in the luxuriant garden of the whole mighty range to the south; it rises like a jagged wall straight up from the broad plain, which spreads in all other directions.

It was over this plain that the Russians came down from the north with their armies and Cossacks in ever greater strength, but were held up at the foot of these mountains; and indeed they have not really got much farther even now. From the plain and up these forest-clad, steep slopes they waged their bloody wars for nearly a hundred years to bring under their yoke the brave, freedom-loving mountain tribes, who defended themselves with an iron heroism, and for every inch of mountain soil took streams of blood. They brought defeat after defeat on the Russian armies, until the fresh on-storming forces were at length too strong in numbers for the small bands of mountain peasants, far worse armed, who in the end had to give in; but rather than become Russian subjects many of them left the land. Not yet did the Caucasus become Russian, and the Russian culture today does not reach much beyond the foot of the mountains.

The wall now lay far behind us there, as a bluish haze—the dividing-line between two worlds, where a hoary antiquity, that still lives, meets our own hurrying times.

Now we had to say farewell to our friend Napoleon, otherwise Narriman Ter Kasarian, our faithful companion throughout the crowded journey from the time when we arrived at Batum, which now seemed so long ago, although it was only a little over three weeks. He was now going back the same way with his Armenian friend and the ladies, and would spend the night in the hotel at Kasbek. We were sad at heart, and felt a deep yearning to go back there, and once more to go through the great adventure in that overwhelming world heaved up and torn asunder by the mightiest cosmic forces in the abysmal depths and on the surface—by the mighty buckling of the earth's crust, by volcanoes and their fiery streams, by the poised glaciers, by the splintering strength of the frost, by the thundering avalanche, by the rushing, wearing masses of water. Gladly would we have spent days, nights, and weeks in this untamed nature on so vast a scale, high up there above all the struggles and pettiness of earthly life.

V

TO DAGHESTAN

TO DAGHESTAN

At four in the afternoon the train left Vladikavkaz, and after half an hour on the short branch line we were at Beslan, which is on the main line from Moscow to Petrovsk and Baku. We had to wait an hour and a half for our train to leave at 6.9 p.m. I spent the time watching the village market just by the station, where peasant women were selling fruit and food: roast fowls, cutlets, bread by weight, and so on. There was a lively traffic, as people were just buying food to take home for the evening. My attention was particularly drawn by a young and beautiful woman who stood there offering her grilled cutlets on a dish, and had a little son with her holding a dish with roast fowls. She may well have seen better days, but she patiently bore with men coming and taking up the cutlets to look at them, and then, having asked the price, putting them back without buying, though some did. The fowls, too, were felt and pinched and put back. It was painful to watch, but at last she got rid of one.

Farther down the street was a tombola, with a woman standing by the round table. Around the edge were all kinds of small things, such as pocket-handkerchiefs and the like. You paid so many kopecks, spun a pointer round in the middle of the table, and the thing opposite which it stopped you took. There was an eager crowd round this table of fortune.

One was struck by seeing women standing here to trade. It was in marked contrast to the world we had come from, where they are seldom seen, even in the Tiflis market-place, and where all trading, both in the market and in the bazaars, is carried on by the men. We were once more in Russia.

Then the express came, and we went eastwards over the plain. We got places in the international *wagon-lit*, and it was like being back in Europe again.

At two in the morning (Tuesday, 7th of July) we reached Petrovsk, or Makhach Kalá as it is called now, after one of the martyrs of the Soviet revolution. This town lies on the Caspian Sea, and is the capital of the autonomous republic of Daghestan. We were cordially greeted by the president of Daghestan himself, Samursky, and by Korkmazov, the president of the government (the commissariat). We were driven in motor-cars to President Samursky's house, where his wife offered tea and refreshments. We were, indeed, welcomed with all the hospitality characteristic of these mountain peoples. The president and his wife, besides his one large office and reception-room, had only three rooms to live in, and one of these, with two good beds, was now given up to Quisling and myself. After our long eventful day we slept like logs in this new world we had now come to.

DAGHESTAN : A SURVEY

The present Autonomous Soviet-Socialist Republic of Daghestan was founded at the time of the

revolution and civil war that ended in 1921.
It governs itself in home affairs, but for other
purposes it is a part of the Russian Soviet-
Socialist Federative Republic, which again, with the
Ukraine, the Trans-Caucasian Republics, White
Russia, the Turkoman Republic, and Uzbegistan,
makes up the great Federation of Soviet-Socialist
Republics.

The Daghestan Republic stretches for 360 kilometres along the west coast of the Caspian Sea from
the river Samur south of Derbent to the river Kuma
in the steppes to the north. The total area is about
54,000 square kilometres. According to President
Samursky's statement the areas of the various
kinds of land in square kilometres are as follows:

	Square Kilometres
Republic of Daghestan	49,660
Bare mountains	17,100
Swamps and reedy land	3,200
Sandy land	3,510
Forest	1,980
Grass-land	10,940
Meadow-land	7,700
Arable land	4,955
Gardens	265

The southern half of the republic is the mountain-
land Daghestan (= rock-land) proper, which
stretches from the coast over the ridges of the
Caucasus south-westwards to the valley of the
Alasán. On the south it marches with Azerbaidjan,
on the south-west with Georgia, on the west northwards of this with Chechnia. This mountain-land
is wild and crossed by lofty ridges with deep

95

narrow valleys between, which—especially in the southern part—mostly run north-west to south-east, parallel with the main direction of the range. In the north of the mountain-land the ridges and valleys to a great extent run north-eastwards (cp. p. 35).

Among the most important rivers in the Daghestan mountains is the Sulak, formed by the junction of the Andian Koisu, the Avarian Koisu (Kara Koisu) and the Kasimukhian Koisu. With its valleys, running north-east and north, this river-basin takes up the whole northern part of the mountain-land. In its southern part the biggest river is the Samur, which with its valleys runs in its upper reaches south-east, and then bends north-eastwards and with its lower reaches makes the boundary with Azerbaidjan. The flat lands in the north of the republic are watered by the river Terek, which with the many arms of its wide delta covers a great area.

While the mountains in Chechnia and its border province Ichkeria are clothed in thick forests, mostly of great beeches—anyhow they were before the Russians partly destroyed them during the war against Shamyl—the valleys and mountains of Daghestan are bare and treeless, but for a few places.

The population of the republic of Daghestan according to the census of 1926 was 788,000, of whom 383,000 were men and 405,000 women. There were 85,000 persons in the bigger towns, and 705,000 settled on the land. The percentages

PAST THE WATERSHED. VIEW OVER THE VALLEY TOWARDS THE KASBEK GROUP

THE FORT IN THE DARIAL GAP

for the most important elements were according to
this census about as follows:

	Per cent.	About
Daghestan mountain tribes (Lesghis)	61·8	487,000
Russians	12·5	98,400
Kumyks	11·2	89,300
Nogaians	3·3	26,000
Chechens	2·3	18,100
Turks (Tatars)	3·0	23,600
Mountain Jews	1·5	11,800
	95·6	754,200

The Town population was made up of:

	Per cent.	About
Russians and Ukrainians	43·5	37,000
Jews	17·1	14,500
Persians	12·9	11,000
Lesghis	9·1	7,700
Tatars	6·3	5,350
Kumyks	4·9	4,160
Armenians	2·0	1,700
Other peoples	4·2	3,570
	100·0	84,980

The Country population was made up of:

	Per cent.	About
Lesghian peoples—		
Avars and Andians	24·0	169,200
Darghis	17·0	119,850
Kurins	13·0	91,700
Lakians (Kasimukhians)	6·3	44,400
Turkish peoples—		
Kumyks	15·0	105,750
Nogaians	5·4	38,070
Turks	3·3	23,270
Chechens	2·7	19,040
Russians and Ukrainians	11·0	77,550
Other peoples	2·3	16,200
	100·0	705,030

G

The figures given show only the approximate distribution. The peoples named speak wholly differing tongues, but each really represents a group of tribes often speaking such different dialects that they can hardly understand one another. According to Samursky there are thirty-two different languages and dialects in Daghestan. The Lesghian peoples make up the mountain tribes in Daghestan proper. The Turkish- (Tatar-) speaking Kumyks dwell on the very edge of the north-east slopes of the mountains, and on the flat land along the Caspian, from the river Rubas, south of Derbent, to north of Petrovsk towards the river Sulak. On the flat land farther north dwell the Turkish Nogaians, and in between along the Terek are Terek Cossacks.

The multitude of tongues gives rise, of course, to many difficulties. Five chief ones are usually named besides Russian. They are: Turkish, Kumykian, Lakian (Kasimukhian), Daghinian, and Avarian. The school instruction is in the first two years given in the mother-tongue, but after this the children have to learn Turski-Kumykian or Russian. In the higher school, after three years Russian is compulsory, and also Kumykian. But both Russian and Turski-Kumykian are far removed from the other languages spoken in the land, besides which, Russian is hated by the people because of the Tsarist government's ruthless policy and russification. There is, moreover, the opposition of the Mohammedan clergy to the giaour tongues. There are now published a Russian, a Kumyk, a Lakian, and an Avar newspaper. The official language in eastern Daghestan is Turski-Kumykian, but in western Daghestan Avarian is mostly used.

The five biggest towns in Daghestan are: Petrovsk, now called Makhach Kalá, Temir-Khan-Shura, now called Buinaksk, Derbent, Kizliar, and Hazaf-Yrt, which, however, was almost wholly destroyed during the civil war.

Where these mountain peoples, the Lesghis and Chechens, came from is unknown to us; and we know little of their prehistory, for they themselves have no records, and are not spoken of by the early historians of other peoples. Their languages, as we have already seen, have so far not yielded any real information; philologists have not been able to find any certain connections. Their heads on the whole are very short and high, the length from the ear to the crown of the head being very great; the face is often of middling length, and in the southern part, where they seem to be least mixed with other peoples, the nose is often long and thin and bent at the end, while the lower part of the face is weak and small. They have brown eyes, dark hair and beard; and usually are of middling height, but often they are tall. In North Daghestan they may also be fair, slender, well made, lithe, and wiry; but where they seem to be least mixed with other peoples the type has a strong likeness to the Armenian-Dinaric racial type, which may show that originally they came from Hither Asia, where in prehistoric and early historic times there seem to have been many peoples with this racial type, which may also have taken to itself Semitic characteristics, although these peoples were not originally Semitic.

The Lesghian tribes live up in the mountain valleys in villages (*a-ul*), which lie in terraces, house above house up the sides of the great mountains, always facing south so as to get the warmth of the sun; they are generally in very inaccessible places, easy to defend. The houses are rectangular, as a rule, built of stone with coarse mortar, and mostly on two floors; they are flat-roofed, and so packed one above the other that the roof of one house often makes a kind of courtyard or terrace for the one over it. It is the same as what we have already (pp. 56, 57, 66) described in the case of Khevsurs and Ossetes. On the lower floor are the stalls and store-rooms, on the upper floor the room for the men and women, and the guest-room. It is seldom that there is a separate room for the women. There are but few chairs; they sit with crossed legs on the ground, which is spread with rugs; sometimes there are also rugs hanging on the walls. As fuel, dried cow-dung in bricks is mostly used, also wood where there is any. The houses are generally separated from the narrow, steep streets by a small courtyard fenced with a stone wall, which has no opening but the gate.

Over their underclothes the men wear a long cloth coat with a belt round the waist, cloth trousers, leather leggings, and soft leather shoes, or else high felt boots. On their head they wear heavy sheep-skin caps; the hair is usually close-cropped. Over the coat they wear a thick cloak (*burka*) of coarse felt, usually without sleeves, or in the higher valleys a long fleecy sheep-skin with a wide shaggy collar; this is often worn over the *burka*. The women wear wide trousers, a shift, and a coat, usually blue, and belt. They wear their hair in plaits, and cover the head with a kind of shawl or a hood hanging down at the sides, and often adorned with coins. In the winter they generally wear felt boots, in the summer they go bare-footed. For weapon the men as a rule carry only the *kindja!* (a big dagger).

They live mostly by cattle-rearing, and keep sheep, goats, cows, buffaloes, horses, and asses. The small cattle are the more important, and especially they have many goats, more than there are in other parts of the Caucasus. For the cattle they find grazing in the mountains in summer, while for the rest of the year the men, often accompanied by women and children, are wont to betake themselves with the cattle down to the flat land by the Caspian, or to the steppes in the north. There is but little agriculture up in the mountains, where the small patches of earth on the ledges have to be fenced with stone walls so as not to be washed away, and the soil must often be carried up. They are artificially watered and yield a rich harvest, but not enough to support the people, and corn and flour have to be brought from the flat land below or from Georgia. Even in good years the harvest is only enough for three or four months' needs. They also do some trout-fishing, and shoot hares, pheasants, and partridges. In Avaria there is also hawking.

Their food is simple: black bread made from barley and beans, cheese, milk, onions, and a kind of noodles made from an unleavened dough of barley, millet, maize, or bean-meal. In winter-time, when the cattle are below on the flats, they eat dried sheep's flesh, as we do in summer when the cattle are up in the mountains. They seldom drink beer; on the other hand, at festivals there may be spirits, must, and wine, in spite of Mohammed's prohibition.

The religion of Daghestan is Islam, which was brought to the Lesghis in the 8th century. They conscientiously keep most of the religious precepts, with prayers, washing, alms, and so forth, and do not seem to have anything left from the original heathen religion of nature. The Chechens, on the other hand, were mostly Christians till the 18th century, when they took over Islam from their neighbours, the Kumyks and Kabardians. Among them are still to be found vestiges of a pre-Christian religion of nature with the worship of various nature gods. In all these tribes Arabic is the religious language, used for reading the Koran. The Soviet government in Daghestan is not so opposed to religion as the Moscow government; rather, it seeks to work along with it. President Samursky says in his book that "the best policy in Daghestan is to make use of the clergy, and in this way slowly build up a secular *intelligentsia*, or intellectual class". The Soviet government had by 1925 set up 93 schools in the country, with 6,951 pupils. The instruction is arranged so that the children first go to an elementary school for three years, then to a higher school for four years. But most of the schools cover only the first grades. In 1923 it was resolved in Moscow that as from 1933-4 there is to be compulsory education in Asia, and this, of course, applies to Daghestan. Besides these government schools there is a far greater number of Mohammedan schools, with over 40,000 pupils, we are told by Samursky, and this he looks upon as a danger, for the resulting Mohammedan influence may become too strong. This is also true of the influence arising from the fact of there being so few national courts of justice in the land, so that the administration of justice falls into the hands of the Mohammedan clergy, which enforces the *shariat* (the holy precepts) instead of the civil law. The government, therefore, is considering the question of setting up new national courts or tribunals; but this again has its difficulties, since the people still remember the Tsarist courts.

It is a curious thing that blood revenge is still widespread in Daghestan, in spite of the fact that it is in opposition to the Koran and the holy precepts, and that Shamyl and the Mohammedan prophets were strongly against it. It is said that 80 per cent. of the murders are still the result of this institution.

Among the Lesghis and the Chechens there is no distinction of rank, although among Lesghian tribes, such as the Avars, Lakians, and others, there were khans ruling wide areas. The relations between the sexes and the division of labour between them are regulated by the holy precepts, as also the institution of marriage. As a rule a man has but one wife, and for her he pays a small sum. But among the Avars the girls are better off; they can choose their own husband, and if a girl goes to the house of the man she has chosen, he has to marry her. Among some mountain-dwellers, after the father's death the eldest son must take over his wives, except his own mother. Others had the same custom as the Great Russians: the father married his son when under age with a grown-up girl, whom he then lived with himself; the children were divided between him and the son when the latter grew up and could take over the wife. Children are often suckled by the mother until five and six years old.

Hospitality is a holy law for these mountaineers. They may attack and rob a stranger on the road for the sake of a small booty, but once he steps over their threshold he is safe, even if he is a foe, and gets food and shelter, while his host will even protect him against others.

The men do the heavy tasks, and the women do the household work, and milk the cattle, mind the children, set the cow-dung cakes to dry, cleanse the wool, spin and weave, fetch water, reap the corn with sickles. The men make the hay, graze the cattle, shear the sheep, plough and till the land, thresh, build the houses, slaughter the cattle, and so on. Among other things the women make woven and knitted carpets of sheep's wool and goat's hair; fine and coarse Lesghian shawls of goat's hair, and sheep's and camel's wool; embroideries of gold and silver

A-UL IN DAGHESTAN (CHOKH)

شامويل

SHAMYL

GUNIB

thread on velvet, silk, and leather; saddle-bags and clothes-bags of carpeting; coarse corn and flour sacks of goat's hair; saddle-cloths and boots of felt or frieze, and so forth.

The Lesghis are often good craftsmen: stone-workers, masons, carpenters, smiths; and among the Kasimukhians especially there are skilful silver- and coppersmiths and weapon-makers. Particularly famous were the weapon-makers of Kubachi, who are often spoken of as early as the 6th century A.D.; their blades and gun-barrels were largely sent to Russia. The most important district for gold- and silversmiths, and for inlay work in steel, ivory, horn, and mother-of-pearl, is that between Kaitago and Tabassaran.

Communications in this wild, riven mountain tract are, of course, difficult; there are only narrow pack-horse roads, which often go up the sheer mountain-sides, high above the streams that fill the narrow valleys. Where the mountain walls are too steep, wooden balks are driven in, and on them are laid lengths of wood and twigs and stones. Small bridges are generally of wood; everything has to be carried on the backs of horses, asses, or men and women.

The conditions of life altogether are uncommonly hard in the valleys between these mighty mountains, and the life there is one of grinding toil; but it rears a rugged, brave, warlike race. They are splendid horsemen, particularly the Chechens, and have extraordinarily good and tough horses, with which they can ride up to 150 kilometres in a day.

They were also skilled in the use of arms and excellent shots.

We must still say a few words about the Kumyks living in the coast-land north and south of Petrovsk and in the most easterly of the mountains inland. They are not to be confused with the Kasimukhians or Lakians, who are a mountain tribe in south-east Daghestan. They speak a Turkish tongue very near akin with that of the Nogaians, their neighbours on the north, and may be in part descendants of the Khazars.

These last make their appearance early in history, and already we find Firdusi using Khazar as a name for the foes of Persia on the north. The home of the Khazars was perhaps the north-eastern and eastern offshoots of the Caucasus, and a district along the Caspian, which latter was called *Bahr-el-Khazar* (=the Khazar Sea) by the Arab geographers of the Middle Ages. Their early capital was Semender, known later as Tarku (near the Makhach Kalá of to-day); it was moved thence to Itil at the mouth of the Volga in the 7th century, after the Mohammedan invasion of Caucasia. It is uncertain who the Khazars were racially, but much seems to point to Ugrian and Turkish connections. For a while they were under Hun dominion (after A.D. 448) and for a while under the Turks (about A.D. 580). That Ugrian people, the Hungarians, were a tribe in their land. The Khazars had a light skin and black hair, and were marked out by a rare beauty of face and form; the women were much sought after as wives both in Byzantium and in Baghdad. Their kingdom, Khazaria, lay between the Caucasus, the Volga, and the Don, but at times stretched much farther. The Khazar culture was relatively high; they founded towns, had a full-grown state system; they were well known for their industry, faithfulness to duty, and trustworthiness—qualities lacking in the Hun character. When their kingdom was destroyed by the Varangian (that is, Scandinavian-Slav) kingdom in Kiev at the end of the 9th and during the 10th century, and the last remnant wiped out in 1016, it may be that a part of the Khazars was left in the district between the lower reaches of the Terek and the Caucasus. Possibly, too, they were joined by bands from Turkish-Tatar tribes that came with the Turks in their wanderings, and with Chingis Khan's (1221) and Tamerlane's (1395) Mongols in the 13th and 14th centuries. The Kumyk rulers, called *shamkhal*, settled in Tarku.

The Kumyks are a peaceful, steady, hard-working, enterprising, and cleanly people. The houses are comparatively roomy—working-rooms below, and above are separate rooms for men and for women, with windows, and an open balcony in front. They are Sunnites, but can also be on good terms with Shiites. They carry on fishery in the Caspian, breed cattle (mostly sheep and horses), and keep bees; they now also carry on some agriculture through irrigation. They are great horsemen, and take wild horses with the lasso, which these fearless riders quickly tame. They are also traders, selling their carpets, sheep's wool, hides, fish, salt, etc., in great quantities to Persia, and getting other wares, which they sell to the Lesghis. The main seat of trade was Tarku, with the harbour which is now Makhach Kalá. They have the aristocratic social system of the steppe-dwellers, with rulers, nobles, commons, and slaves.

From the economic standpoint the Daghestan peoples have great difficulties now to fight against. The possibilities of the land have never been developed to any satisfactory degree. For this capital is needful, and so it cannot easily be done without State help. The Tsarist government seems to have been more concerned with russifying the land than with helping on its industries and developing its economic possibilities. Then came the war and the civil war, and economic conditions throughout the land were seriously affected; railways, telegraphs, shipping, etc., were destroyed; 75 per cent. of the cattle disappeared; of the vineyards three-fourths were destroyed; the fisheries suffered dreadfully; and there were other afflictions. Then came the cattle pest in 1922, a plague of field-mice in the same year which destroyed the crops, bad crops in 1924, and so on. Altogether there were 3,600,400 head of cattle in 1911, but in 1923 only 1,480,000.

Added to these economic difficulties is the fact that the health of the country is not good. Malaria is widespread, especially in the lowland, where a heavy percentage of the people suffers from it. Venereal diseases are also rife; the workers bring them from the towns when they come back to their *a-ul.* There are only very few doctors, especially in the mountains; and even where there are any, little use is made of them. The men, indeed, go to them, but the women are afraid, and will not trust themselves to them.

The economic position being so difficult, and there being so little land in the mountain valleys, many of the men (Samursky says 200,000) leave the country every autumn after the harvest to seek work in other parts of Caucasia, in Turkestan, and also in places inside Russia; they come back again in the spring. Many thousands come to Baku to work. Samursky believes this is of great importance economically for Daghestan, and also culturally, through European culture being brought into the mountains. But it has its drawbacks, and especially does it have a demoralizing effect on the people through bringing in venereal diseases and alcoholism.

The Daghestan government has tried all it can with its scanty means to improve trade and industry. It has made a great irrigation canal, and built new roads; it has, so far as it could, granted credit for buying cattle, and given much care and thought to improving its fisheries, and granted credit to them also. The government has also sought to build up new industries by starting cotton-spinning, glass-working, and so on.

There are, indeed, many openings, if only capital could be found. There is water-power in plenty for electrification; a commission of engineers has examined into the question, but so far it has not been possible to do anything. Samursky points out that the buying and selling of the products will be made considerably easier through the co-operative movement; this organization now has 13,000 members, or other families.

In Makhach Kalá

In the morning of the 7th of July I took a stroll through the town. My first goal was the Caspian Sea; I sought it through the streets, and so down to the shore. There it lay, stretching away towards the horizon, a glorious blue under the fresh breeze in the morning sunshine. But not a sail, not a ship, not a boat was there to see on the broad blue surface. Along the low sandy shore were strewn yellow-brown clusters of bathing boys. There was no essential difference to be seen between this, the world's greatest inland sea, and the sea in general— anyhow, at first sight. True, the shore had no marks of ebb and flow, as we know them; but then there are none in the Mediterranean or the Black Sea. It is not to be wondered at, therefore, that when the old Greeks heard of this mighty lake with salt water, they took it to be an inlet of the Okeanos girdling the whole inhabited world, although Herodotus held it to be an enclosed sea.

As is well known, the surface of the Caspian lies slightly below the sea-level, and 26 metres lower than the Black Sea. The average salt-content is about 1·4 per cent., less than half of the average for sea-water, which is about 3·5 per cent. But in shallow, land-locked inlets, where evaporation is heavy, the salt-content is far greater—in the Kara-bugas gulf, for instance, it is 17 per cent.

When I came back to the house my host and hostess were there, and we had a pleasant breakfast with Samursky and Korkmazov. Our hostess poured out coffee, and there was fresh caviare, new-laid eggs, excellent Daghestan cheese. It could not have been better. But unfortunately I spoke neither Turkish nor Russian, and all my conversation with Samursky and his wife had to be carried on through Quisling as an interpreter in Russian, or through Korkmazov, who spoke French excellently.

Language conditions in Daghestan are, as I said above, very complicated. The official language, as spoken by Samursky and Korkmazov, is Turski-Kumyk; but they both spoke Russian also.

Samursky was a comparatively young man, and evidently sprung from the people; he is not very highly educated, and does not seem to be much interested in general literature, but to be all the more interested in practical life. He did not know any of the Western European languages, but published a book in 1925 in Russian on Daghestan. He is a clever man, and undoubtedly a good speaker, and evidently has great influence among the people here. He is a Lesghi from southern Daghestan, his mother-tongue being Lesghian. His real name is Effendi; Samursky is an assumed one. He had no part in the revolutionary movement before the Revolution. For several years he was president of the Central Executive Committee of Daghestan. Now (1929) he is working on the

Russian Economic Council in Moscow. His appearance is striking, and only slightly European: he is of middling height, or short, strongly built, somewhat short-necked, and with a decided broad head. The very remarkable shape of his head was further stressed by the hair being close-cropped, as is usual among the Lesghis. It reminded me strongly of the Armenian type, with a line rising straight up from the nape of the neck with no occiput, a high crown, and a great length from the ears upwards; the forehead is high and retreating, the nose slightly aquiline, and the mouth and chin retreating—a shape of head which is quite usual among many of the Caucasian tribes. The face was clever, with an almost jovial expression, clean-shaven, and of middling length; the forehead was comparatively narrow, the eyes wide apart, and the mouth very firm.

Korkmazov is a Kumyk from Kum-Tor-Kale, near Makhach Kalá; he is more European-looking. The alert face is broader, as is the forehead; the hair is gray and curly. He is older, a little bigger and taller than the other fellow. His mother-tongue is Turski-Kumyk, the most widespread language in Daghestan, and, along with Russian, the official one. He is highly intelligent, and is well educated; a lawyer by profession, he is well read; he was a revolutionary and before the Revolution lived some time as a fugitive in Paris.

Makhach Kalá is a town of some 30,000 inhabitants. It was founded in 1844, after the Russian fort of Nizovoe, three kilometres away, had been destroyed the year before in the war with Shamyl.

SAMURSKY, PRESIDENT OF THE REPUBLIC OF DAGHESTAN

PRESIDENTS SAMURSKY AND KORKMAZOV

MOUNTAIN LANDSCAPE IN DAGHESTAN

GARDEN AND MOUNTAIN GAP IN DAGHESTAN

It was named Petrovsk, after Peter the Great, who on his unfortunate campaign against the Persians came there on the 12th of August, 1722, made an imposing entry into Tarku, the capital of the Kumyk ruler (*shamkhal*), and went back three days later to his camp on the shore. Here he laid some stones together, and his followers added more, so that there was a heap on the spot where the town was built over a hundred years later. Next day he marched at the head of his army to Derbent, whence he soon had to go back home, as his fleet and transports, that were to follow him, were destroyed by a storm; on the 13th of December he once more triumphantly marched into Moscow.

Petrovsk is now named after a man who fought against the rule of the Tsars. Here was the harbour earlier of the town of Tarku (Tarki), which lies inland about four kilometres to the south. The harbour of Makhach Kalá is now sheltered by two long moles.

Our first visit was to the museum, which gave an insight into the life of the mountain peoples. They are, as we said, Mohammedans and mostly Sunnites, and so have stronger ties with the Turks than with the Persians; but there are also Shiites among them. The Murid movement was partly directed to reconciling the two doctrines and uniting Islam once more, as will be related below. Fanaticism now seems to have died down, and religion has taken on a more modern form, anyhow so far as we saw in this town and its neighbourhood. The women did not wear a veil in the street or in the house, and did not seem to be much afraid of being seen by men. The men seemed mostly to be satisfied with one wife. They plant the vine and drink wine, although Muridism strove against it. On the whole we did not in these respects remark any difference from the usual attitude and customs of Europeans. We did not hear any *muezzin* in this town calling out the times for prayer, and we did not see the men worshipping, or, for instance, saying their evening prayer at sunset, which is generally held to be indispensable for a true Mussulman. It may be that Bolshevism, which seeks to do away with all religion, has had some influence in this.

The museum was to a great extent given up to the history of Daghestan. In particular, it seemed to be a shrine to the memory of Shamyl, the prophet and bitter foe of Russia, with pictures and photographs from his remarkable life, his sabre, his harness, the bag in which he carried the Koran with him, and the cover of the book, the great stars of the order with which he rewarded his brave Murids, and other relics.

Korkmazov spoke to us eloquently of his romantic life, and of how, as Mohammed's unswerving prophet, he had such remarkable power over the mountaineers. He told us, too, of the hero Hadji Murad from Avaria, who for eleven years was an ally of Shamyl and his best leader, defeating the Russians in battle after battle. But Shamyl, who had had a hand in murdering his brother and his near friends, the khans of Avaria, was afraid of him, and in the end was bent on taking his life. To revenge himself Hadji Murad then fled to the Russians. His was a wonderfully tragic figure, torn between his religious hatred for the unbelieving Russian oppressors on the one hand, and on the other his duty of blood revenge and his hatred for Shamyl, who held his family in his power, and was threatening to kill them. They also had here a beautifully illustrated edition of Tolstoi's book on Hadji Murad.

As we went through these rooms, where Shamyl's earnest, brooding countenance spoke to us from the walls, and as the eye wandered through the windows away over the house-tops and plain spread under the burning sun towards those blue mountains that once were the free home of these peoples—our thoughts went back to their shifting history, and to this ruthlessly strong man, this prophet and warrior-leader, who for twenty-five years kept them under his more than human power in an unbroken, relentless struggle against the Russian armies, which, ever growing, attacked him from every side, until, betrayed and forsaken, he was still holding out with a few faithful followers on the top of Mount Gunib, but in the end had to surrender (1859).

From times of old the life of these mountain tribes has been one of fighting, feuds, and robbery. They know how to fight, but find it hard to surrender, as the Russians learned nearly every time they tried to take their *a-ul*.

When in 1832 the Russians stormed the Chechen *a-ul* of Ghermentshuk, there were in the end only three houses still untaken, where a number of Chechens were putting up an embittered resistance and would not yield. At length the Russians managed to set fire to the houses; and their commander now sent an interpreter to the defenders offering peace on favourable conditions. They ceased firing, listened to the proposals, and deliberated for a few minutes; then a smoke-blackened, half-naked Chechen came out and spoke: "We wish for no peace from the Russians; the only grace we ask of them is that they let our families know that we died as we lived, and refused to submit to the foreign yoke." These words were followed by a volley from the whole band. The Russians now opened fire with their guns, and soon the houses were wrapped in flames. The sun had set, and the awful scene of destruction and death was lit up only by the red gleam of the flames, while the Chechens sang their death-song, first loud, then sinking lower and lower, as the houses burned down. At length the walls fell in, and 72 Chechens met their death there.

One of the Chechens' death-songs describes Hamzad's last fight. With a band of horsemen from Ghikh he had been on a plundering expedition over the Terek into the Russian territory, but on his way home he was overtaken by an outnumbering force of Russians. Hamzad and his men slaughtered the plundered horses and cattle, made a breastwork of them, and entrenched themselves behind it. The Russians sent Prince Kagherman to parley with them and get them to surrender; but Hamzad answered:[1] "I came not here, O Kagherman, for want of money; I came to win the death of the

[1] Translation as given by J. P. Baddeley, *The Russian Conquest of the Caucasus* (London, 1908), pp. 487–8.

Ghazavát. And were I to surrender to thee, all the people of Ghikh would laugh me to scorn.

"As a wolf tired and hungry longs to reach the forest, as a horse unfed and mettlesome the fresh clean meadow—so do my companions thirst for the fight unto death. Nor do I fear thee, Kagherman; I laugh at all thy force; for our hope is in God, the All-powerful."

And again Hamzad said to Kagherman: "Ever we sought booty and gold, but for such a day as this there is nothing so precious as the beautiful black powder."

And again he said: "Gold is not money today; today the trusty Crimean flint is pure gold."

Kagherman went back to the Russian commander and told him that Hamzad refused to surrender. And Hamzad returned to his rampart and sat down with his companions.

Then the troops came up and began firing; and Hamzad and his riders fired back.

Thick was the smoke of their firing, and Hamzad said: "May this day be accursed! So hot it is, that we have no shade but that of our swords."

And again he said: "How thick is the smoke, how dark the day! Our only light is the flash of our guns."

And again Hamzad said to his companions: "The Houris of Paradise look down on us from their windows in Heaven and wonder; they dispute together whose they shall be; and she who falls to the braver of us will vaunt it before her friend —and she who falls to the less brave will blush for shame; she will close the lattice on him and turn away; and if any of you plays the coward this day may his face be black when he stands before God!"

But Hamzad thought in his heart the while that death was upon him; he could hope no more.

High in the heavens he saw the birds flying and called to them: "O birds of the air! Give our last greeting, our ultimate salutation, to the Naïb of Ghikh, Akhverdi Mahomá. Greet also from us the beautiful ones, the damsels fair, and tell them that our proud breasts serve to stop Russian bullets —tell them that our wish was to rest after death in the graveyard at Ghikh, where our sisters would have wept on our tombs, and all the people would have sorrowed—but God grants no such grace. Not the sobbing of our sisters will be heard above us, but the howling of famished wolves. Not relations in troops will gather round, but a flock of ravens swart.

"And tell them too, on the Tcherkess hill, in the land of the Giaour, bare blades in hand, we lie dead. The ravens pick out our eyes, the wolves tear our flesh."

The picture this description gives us of the way of thinking and views on life of this people is confirmed by the whole of their history. Should not a people of such metal as this be useful for something higher and greater than war and destruction?

We shall reach a still better understanding of these mountain peoples from a short account of that religious movement known as Muridism, which brought the mountain tribes of Daghestan and the Chechens together, and raised them up against the Russians, and of their heroic and stubborn struggle against superior numbers.

VI

MURIDISM AND THE FIGHT FOR FREEDOM

MURIDISM AND THE FIGHT FOR FREEDOM

When in 1801 the Tsar of Russia had taken to himself the crown of Georgia, it became of great importance to subdue the mountaineers—mostly Mohammedans—in the Caucasus lying between, so as to make the Russian power in the south quite secure. The object was to allow the Tsar to stretch his grasping hand towards the Turks in the south-west and the Persians in the south-east and, indeed, further still, towards India. These mountain peoples were not in great numbers, and could doubtless be overcome without any great difficulty by the huge Russian forces. True, they had done no injury to Russia, and this country had no right whatever to their land, but this had no weight against an Imperial wish; their land had to be made an integral part of the Russian Empire, and free or autonomous tribes in these mountains, or on the plains north of them, "were incompatible with the dignity or honour of the Tsar". What the conquest was to cost in streams of blood, in devastation, want, misery, and suffering for tens of thousands of mountain dwellers was, needless to say, of little weight; this was these people's own fault for setting themselves up against the Imperial commands. Moreover, so it was said, they carried on robbery, took cattle, and plundered people on the high-roads. But what shall one say of the Russian Tsar and his people, who by no right whatever forced their way into their valleys, killed them right and left, plundered their villages (*a-ul*), and seized their whole land?

At the beginning it looked as if all would be comparatively easy for the Russians. The nominally Christian Ossetes and the Christian Georgian mountain tribes (Khevsurs, Pshavs, Tushes, and Shvans or Svanetians) were either not hostile, or else even joined the Russians. This was of very great importance, since they controlled the military road through the Caucasus to Georgia. It is true they now and then practised robbery, or revolted against the oppressors; but this was of no very great importance. The Kabardians on the northern side of the mountains and on the plain both sides of the river Terek, north-west and west of Vladikavkaz, were, of course, Mohammedans, but their land, Kabardia, had been quickly captured by the Russians, and occupied by numerous forts and Cossack *stanitsas* (villages), so that they had to keep themselves quiet. On the other hand, the Cherkesses on the mountain slopes farther west, and the Abkhasians towards the Black Sea, were bitter foes against the Russians, as also were the many Mohammedan tribes in the eastern Caucasus. But both the Chechens in Chechnia and the Lesghis in Daghestan were split up into many tribes of differing tongues, between whom was no national feeling, nay, who were partly hostile to one another. The small Chechen tribes had a highly democratic system with no regular leaders, and were therefore weak at a united defence. Most of the tribes in Daghestan had, as was said above, khans ruling over their own districts, and so they could raise stronger forces.

But owing to the want of union among the tribes the Russians were able to attack them one by one; sometimes, too, they could make friends with some of the tribes and khans, and to some extent play them off against the others. In this wise the Russians in the first period succeeded in making a considerable advance, and in establishing themselves at several important points. This was especially so after General Yermolov took over the command in Georgia and the Caucasus in 1816. He set methodically to work, and attacked one khanate after the other; when the most important parts of Daghestan had submitted, he thought he could report in 1820 to the Tsar: "The Conquest of Daghestan, begun last year, has now been carried to its end; and this land, proud, warlike, and hitherto unvanquished, has fallen before the sacred feet of your Imperial Majesty."

Although it was only an inner western strip of Daghestan that the Russians had not reached, Yermolov's announcement was to prove indeed over-hasty. It was still to cost thirty-nine years' bitter fighting with streams of blood before Daghestan should be overcome. Yermolov's hard and cruel treatment of the inhabitants, the plunder and destruction of their villages (a-ul) by him, and the putting of the inhabitants to the sword, gave rise to a burning hatred of the Russians, and to a craving for freedom which yielded a fruitful soil for a fanatical anti-Russian religious movement, and brought the tribes together in a united resistance.

The strength of Islam had been greatly weakened through the split into two sects: the Sunnites, to which the Turks belonged, and the Shiites, whose doctrines the Persians had adopted. The new doctrine, which soon won the upper hand in the mountain valleys of Daghestan, had for one of its objects the uniting once more of these two sects, and the strengthening of Islam to wage a war of extermination against the unbelievers.

In the *a-ul* (village) of Yaragh in south Daghestan there was living at the beginning of last century a highly respected, kindly old judge called Mullah-Mohammed. He was a mild, peace-loving, wise man of good deeds, and in the course of long nights he had searched the Koran and holy books, which he expounded to the people. He was loved and venerated by all, and they came in crowds to hear him. And so one day Allah's message came to open his eyes, and the peaceful man saw to his horror what a dreadful sin it was to submit to the unbelievers instead of wiping them off the face of the earth. By day and by night he brooded, and then in 1824 he stood out before the people, that was gathered together in great numbers, and spoke of the greatest thing of all—the faith of their fathers; and in his hearers was lit, as it were, a flaming fire. He showed that according to the word of the Prophet no Mussulman must be subject to an unbeliever, and how all acts of penance, purifications, and offerings are of no avail so long as a

Muscovite's eye falls on them; "nay, so long as the Muscovites dwell among you, the Koran is a curse unto you, instead of a blessing". He preached a holy war against unbelievers. He that would share in the eternal blessings of the other world must, according to the words of the Prophet, yield up his life and his belongings for the sake of Allah; he must leave wives and children behind, and throw himself into the fight. Only in this wise can he cross the bridge El-Sirat into Paradise. Here below our hours are told like those of the day, but yonder above, life is everlasting; our true home is there. "Black-eyed Houris, whose eyes are like gleaming stars and arms like swans' necks, will smile on us, but not each and all will they clasp to themselves; fountains with diamond-like water gush out of milk-white marble, but not all shall be refreshed by them; slender cypresses and leafy plane-trees wave their coolness to us, but not all shall rest in their shade"; for he only that goes to the fight to spread the Prophet's teaching and break the unbeliever's power can come unto the blissful state of the chosen. Keep armed, so as to be ready when the hour strikes, calling to the fight!

These words of the old, wise man, born of a glowing hatred for the unbeliever, and calling them to a relentless warfare against the Russians, made a deep impression; the new doctrine quickly spread through Daghestan, where a hatred for the cruel oppressors was already flaming in their hearts. The movement also reached Chechnia, where Russian cruelty and destruction had aroused a

serious rising in 1824 and 1825. The apostles consecrated and blessed by Mullah-Mohammed were
called *murids*, that is, disciples, from the Arabic
word *murid* = "one that seeks" (that is, to find
the way). With burning zeal they preached the
doctrine, and the battle-cry was: "War against
the unbelievers! death to the Russians!" What
appealed to the people, too, was that Muridism
preached the absolute equality of all mankind;
according to the Koran none could be subject to
another. Muridism, moreover, preached a reconciliation between Sunnites and Shiites, who were
all children of God.

Many places were seething, and the movement
was a serious danger for the Russians; their efforts
to stifle it did but add fuel to the fire. The cry was:
Shame and disgrace on you so long as your temples
are profaned by the red-haired Muscovites. Of a
truth it were better that ye pulled down your
temples so as to bury them that mock God under
the ruins. Every stone wherewith ye crush the head
of an unbeliever becomes a monument to the
glory of Allah. And Mullah-Mohammed spoke to
the leaders of the people: "Death or victory! On
the one side Paradise beckons, on the other freedom.
What, then, are we waiting for? Fight, and you are
free, die and you are blessed. Hatred and the sword!
Let the bodies of your slain foes be the steps up
which ye climb to the joys of Paradise; for thus does
the Prophet speak: 'He that slays an unbeliever, his
name shall be praised; but he that falls in the fight
for the faith, his glory shall be great indeed.'"

But a leader was still lacking who should gather and lead the people in war. Then did Mullah-Mohammed lay his hands in blessing on the young Kasi-Mullah from Ghimri in Avaria, and consecrate him to "band the people together and in Allah's name begin the holy war. Paradise awaits him that falls or that slays a Russian; but woe to him that turns his back upon the Giaours!"[1]

This was in 1826, and the fiery Kasi-Mullah, supported by the young Mullah-Shamyl, who was also from Ghimri, at once set about his task. He went from place to place to plant Muridism firmly among the Lesghis and the Chechens, and to bring the people together for the fight. While the Russians were taken up with the war against the Persians and the Turks, he had a fairly clear field; and he was chosen as *imam*, that is, the leader of the people in all spiritual and temporal matters. The greater part of Daghestan was gradually won over; but the Khan of Avaria, in the town of Khunsakh, had not joined him. The quarrelsome inhabitants of this town had no wish to put themselves under the strict laws of Muridism. With an army of some 6,000 men Kasi-Mullah marched from Ghimri against Khunsakh in February 1830. The khan was a minor, and the government was in the hands of his mother, Pakhu-Bikhé. The town of over 700 houses was in an inaccessible position beside a high precipice, and was strongly fortified by breastworks and towers. She thus thought she could hold it. The Murids, in two divisions, one led by

[1] "Giaour" (written "Giaur" by Byron) is the foreign unbeliever.

Kasi-Mullah himself, the other by Shamyl, rushed forward with the war-cry: "Allah-Akbar, lia-il-allahu!" ("God is great, there is no god but God!") At the sight of these yelling ranks already sure of victory, the defenders, who had never before seen or heard anything of the kind, were overcome with fear and began to waver. Then the towering figure of Pakhu-Bikhé put herself at their head with drawn sword and flaming eyes. "Avars," she shouted, "you are not worthy of bearing arms. If you are afraid, hand them over to us women, and save yourselves behind our skirts!" Goaded by these scornful words, the defenders rallied just as the foe came swarming over the breastworks, and they drove them back with heavy losses. The Avars who had joined the Murids now withdrew, and these latter were put to flight, leaving 200 dead, many wounded, and 60 prisoners. Shamyl was for a time in great danger of being killed by his excited fellows, but was saved by a dervish. This was the first of his many dangerous rescues, which to the superstitious mountain-dwellers were a proof that he was Allah's chosen one for carrying out his work on earth. Hadji Murad, who afterwards became so well known and was to be so dangerous an opponent for the Russians, gathered up the banners and ensigns left behind by the Murids on the battlefield, and sent them to Tiflis as proof of the Avars' faithfulness towards Russia. Kasi-Mullah withdrew in confusion with his men to Ghimri, and proclaimed that this sad defeat was Allah's punishment on the people for their lack of faith and their ways of uncleanness. Withal, his influence was naturally greatly weakened, but it was soon strengthened again by his success in the struggle against the Russians.

The Russians, having brought the war with Persia and Turkey to an end, turned again in strength against the tribes in the Caucasus, and in 1830 tried to force a way with their troops into Daghestan and Chechnia; but in the brave and daring Kasi-Mullah they found a dangerous opponent. Although he might at times be defeated by them and their guns, of which he had none, or withdraw, luring them on into the mountains or into the dense forests of Chechnia, he would soon fall on them unexpectedly from another side, and inflict one bloody defeat after another on them. In May 1831 he destroyed Paraul, where the Kumyk Shamkhal was quartered, and took his capital, Tarku, right under the Russian guns in the fortress of Burnaya commanding the town. He then laid siege to the fortress itself, and came near to taking it, when it was relieved, and he once more withdrew. But soon after, in June, he advanced again, and besieged the strong fortress of Vnezapnaya in the plain to the north. Upon a Russian army hastening up he withdrew into the forests, and when the Russians followed him up he inflicted a bloody defeat on them, Emanuel himself, the Russian general, being wounded.

In August of the same year he even laid siege for a week to the fortified town of Derbent on the Caspian, until it was relieved; while in November he suddenly made a bold attack on the town and fort of Kizliar, far to the north on the plain of the lower Terek and near its delta. The town was plundered, and Kasi-Mullah came back to Daghestan with 200 prisoners, mostly women, and a great booty.

But soon his star was to come to its setting. On the 1st of December the Russians stormed his fortified headquarters at Shumkeskent (Agach-Kalá), in the forest-clad mountains in north-eastern Daghestan. Kasi-Mullah fled, but the Russians suffered heavy losses.

As characteristic of the mountaineers' method of fighting, a little incident near the mountain of Gai may be related from this time. The Galgais, a small Chechen tribe in the mountains near the Georgian military road, were making this unsafe, and had to be punished. A Russian army with infantry, cavalry, and mountain guns advanced into their mountain valleys without meeting any strong resistance. One day the Russians were marching along a narrow path on a steep mountain slope. Suddenly they found the way barred before them by a strong stone tower on an inaccessible crag. From it the enemy was firing with deadly aim; the small Russian three-pounders had but little effect, and could not break down the door of thick oak planks, which was the height of three men above the ground, without any stair or ladder. A footpath was found leading over the mountain past the tower; it was impracticable for the horses and baggage, but two companies climbed up it and the tower was surrounded. The defenders were called upon to surrender, but refused. As the guns were of no use a mine had to be laid under the tower. After three days' siege and work the mine was laid, and the tower could now be blown up; but first of all the humane Russian general, von Rosen, once more sent a messenger to the defenders to get them to surrender. They now made answer that they would come, but must have two hours to take away the stones that were piled up behind the heavy oak door. When the time was up, the general, with his whole staff and a company of sharpshooters at the ready, took up their position before the tower to receive the prisoners. The door was opened; first half a dozen muskets were handed out, then two tattered and grimy men lowered themselves down by a rope. They folded their arms and scowled at the Russians, awaiting their lot.

"What has become of the others?" asked the general impatiently.

"We were only two," the prisoners answered.

In April 1832 Kasi-Mullah was bold enough to threaten Vladikavkaz itself, and to besiege the fortress of Nazran on the plain by the river Sundja, north-east of the town. He hoped in this way to get the Kabardians to rise. For some days things looked bad for the Russians, but he then withdrew again. In August the Russians invaded Chechnia with success; they took the largest and wealthiest *a-ul* (village) there, Ghermenchuk, whose inhabitants put up an heroic defence, although most of them had no firearms (cp. p. 115). Kasi-Mullah withdrew into Daghestan, and, followed by the faithful Shamyl, he fortified himself in the end in his native town of Ghimri; but many of his followers had now lost hope and fallen away.

In October 1832 the Russians advanced against Ghimri. The approach was extraordinarily difficult, scarred with ravines and deep precipices. When it was said that the road was impassable for troops, the Russian commander-in-chief, General Veliaminov, asked: "Can a dog make its way along this road?" When they answered: "Well, perhaps a dog could." "That's enough!" said he. "Where a dog can go, a Russian soldier can, too." About six kilometres above and beyond the town Kasi-Mullah and Shamyl had built a threefold wall in the gorge, with a stone breastwork at the side; and here the enemy had to get through. Near the outer wall were two small stone houses. It cost the Russians a bitter struggle to take this position, and both sides fought heroically. When the first attempt to storm the outer wall failed, General Veliaminov had a drum brought up, on which he sat down, and quite calmly began to examine the enemy's position through his glass. The defenders soon caught sight of him, and the bullets whistled round him; men fell right by his side. The Prince of Mingrelia, who was in command of a regiment, begged the general to come farther away. Veliaminov calmly answered him: "Yes, Prince, it is indeed a dangerous spot; will you, therefore, be so good as to lead your regiment at once against the breastworks there on the right." In the end the defenders were driven from the walls and breast-works; but in the two stone houses some sixty Murids kept up the defence, and would not give in. The houses were bombarded and stormed by the Russians. The defenders neither asked for quarter nor accepted it; they rushed out in twos and fours seeking to cut their way through, and died fighting; only two men escaped. A tall, slender figure showed itself on the high threshold of the doorway; but as the soldiers raised their guns to fire he leaped over their heads and alighted behind them; he turned and in a flash cut down three of them, but got a bayonet right through his breast; he caught hold of it with one hand, cut down his assailant, drew the bayonet out of his own breast, and slipped away into the forest, in spite of also having a rib and shoulder broken by a stone. None knew him, but it was Shamyl.

Among the many dead lying before the two stone houses there was a remarkable figure which in death had taken up the attitude of a Mussulman at prayer, with his left hand about his beard and the right lifted towards the sky. When the natives came up they recognized their *imam*, Kasi-Mullah. The Russians rejoiced, and exposed the body, but the mountaineers were gloomy: his attitude in death, with the hand pointed upwards, showed him to be a holy man, and he had died in the great cause.

Next day the Russians could march into Ghimri without meeting any resistance. They now believed

that Muridism was definitively overcome, and that
the Russian dominion in Daghestan was assured.
They had not taken into account that Shamyl had
got away and was perhaps still alive, nor the
impression Kasi-Mullah's heroic death had made
upon his followers.

After three days without food Shamyl managed
to reach Untsukul, near the Koisu, south of Ghimri.
Here for twenty-five days he lay between life and
death, for the Russian bayonet had gone through
one of his lungs; and for many months more his
life was in danger before he was fully recovered.
That he escaped at Ghimri in some wonderful way
unknown to anyone was for his people a fresh and
sure sign that he was Allah's chosen one.

While Shamyl lay sick Mullah-Mohammed consecrated Hamzad-Beg as *imam* and leader in the
holy war (*ghazavat*). He also was from Avaria—
from Gotsatl, near Khunsakh. He had joined Kasi-
Mullah, and at times fought along with him, but
had not his qualities; at Ghimri he had failed him
to save his own skin. With Shamyl's help he succeeded in strengthening Muridism and securing
his own power. Most of Avaria had also joined him,
but not the Khan of Khunsakh. In August 1834,
therefore, he marched against the town in great
strength. Pakhu-Bikhé, who understood that this
time resistance was bootless, was minded to adhere
to Muridism, but not to the *ghazavat*; she sent her
youngest son, Bulach Khan, eight years old, to
Hamzad as a hostage. By fair promises Hamzad also
lured the two elder sons, Abu-Nuntsal and Umma

(Omar), to his camp to negotiate; then, egged on by Shamyl, this faithless breaker of his promises had them both murdered, together with some of their following. First Umma Khan was killed; then the eldest brother, Abu-Nuntsal, fell "like a raging lion" on his foes, and he is said by eye-witnesses to have killed twenty of the Murids before he was brought down by his many wounds. Hamzad-Beg was now able to march into Khunsakh, and here he had the Khans' mother, Pakhu-Bikhé, beheaded, although she had taken him into her house when he was young and treated him like a son. Abu-Nuntsal's widow was spared since she was with child; she bore a son, who later became Khan of Avaria.

But Hamzad-Beg's treacherous deed did harm to his reputation, and the Avars, who were attached to their khans, fell away from him. Hadji Murad and his brother Osman, being foster-brothers and near friends to the dead khans, had the duty of taking blood revenge, and during a religious festival in the mosque at Khunsakh on Friday, the 19th of September, 1834, they killed Hamzad-Beg right in the midst of his Murids. Osman was killed, but Hadji Murad got away. The people rose in revolt, the Murids fled, and Hadji Murad became leader in Avaria.

Shamyl was not in Khunsakh when this happened. As soon as he got news of it, he gathered a force together and marched to Gotsatl. There he took the treasury and made Hamzad's uncle hand over the boy Bulach Khan, whom he, Shamyl, had strangled and thrown down a mountain into the Avarian Koisu. The old Mullah-Mohammed was now dead, and after Hamzad-Beg's death Shamyl was chosen at Ashilta as *imam* and leader of the Murids. He was beyond compare the most important of them all.

VII

SHAMYL

SHAMYL

Shamyl, perhaps one of the most remarkable figures of the century, was born in 1797 at Ghimri in Avaria, on the Avarian Koisu near where it meets the Andian Koisu. His name was Ali, but later he was called Shamyl (that is, Samuel).[1] He was, to an extraordinary degree, a born leader of men, and richly endowed by nature. Physically, he was fairly tall, slender, and with a proud bearing. His eyes were blue or gray, his hair and beard blond with a touch of brown, his face fairly long and narrow with regular features, and an earnest, thoughtful, and calm expression. In a simple and dignified garb with a belt round his waist, and usually without any of the glowing colours affected by his Murids or any gold and silver, his figure always made a deep impression on his people, and his movements were careful and dignified. He excelled at sports, and was first in fencing, running, jumping, and all kinds of gymnastic exercises. It was said of him that he could leap a ditch 27 feet wide (?), and could jump higher than his own height. As a young man he went bare-legged and bare-breasted in all kinds of weather, and stood out even among the Daghestan mountaineers for his daring and powers of endurance.

He was gifted with a sharp understanding,

[1] The proper pronunciation is *Shamwil* (*i* long, and the *w* with a slight *u* sound). As Shamyl is the form generally used it is kept here.

capacity for organization, inventiveness, shrewd-
ness, extraordinary strength of will and self-control,
and unswerving courage, and he was a great
military leader. He had a fiery eloquence and
enthusiasm, linked with shrewd calculation. He
knew his own people, and always understood the
right thing to say and to do. A remarkable reader
of men, he knew how to make full use of their good
and of their bad side. Like most great leaders, he
was an excellent actor; and through his calmness,
his pious, prophet-like bearing, his ascetic life, his
way of keeping in the background, so that people
seldom saw him, and his long lonely wrestling
with the Prophet and Allah, he wrapped himself
in the mystical glory of Allah's chosen one and
Mohammed's vicar, winning an extraordinary
sway over men's minds. Besides this he had a varied
knowledge, and had read deeply in the Koran
and the holy books, as also in the Christian Gospel,
which he applied to the revision of his own doctrine.
He well knew how to make use of all this knowledge;
his glowing proclamations to the peoples were often
true masterpieces.

But also he could be crafty and cruel, ruthlessly
severe towards his own, if they did not blindly
yield to his will; and he made himself feared through
his gruesome punishments and death-sentences.
Thieves he punished by cutting off their hands,
and small offences were often punished with death.
The penalties were always enjoined on him by
Allah, whose prophet he was, and in whose name,
as *imam*, the all-powerful dispenser of everything

spiritual and temporal, he wrote his laws after his own will and could alter the precepts of Sharshat as he chose. His words and promises were therefore not always to be trusted; and towards prisoners of war his behaviour was often cruel and showed scant nobility.

Always, even in the greatest danger, he was fully master of himself, and he passed the cruellest sentences of punishment and death as calmly as he praised and rewarded meritorious deeds. But this stern man had also his milder side; he was a tender son, husband, and father, and could show a touching love for children, and delight in being with them.

Although the Russians once more thought they had wholly broken down the mountaineers' resistance, this new leader was to hold his own against mighty Russia for twenty-five years. With his comparatively few followers he defeated the Russians time after time; and each time they thought they at last had him in their grasp, he slipped through their hands mysteriously, and attacked them soon again from another side. It was as though he were in league with supernatural powers.

When he became leader the position seemed almost hopeless. After Hamzad-Beg's murder of the Khans and his own death, most of Avaria, as was said above, fell away, led on by Hadji Murad. Many other tribes did the same; but as if by a miracle Shamyl succeeded in putting life into Muridism again, and gathering the people around him. He marched against Khunsakh, but was beaten by the rugged Hadji Murad. Shamyl once more tried to take the town, but soon had to turn against the Russians, who were advancing from other directions. In the end, in October 1834, he was defeated by the capable and brave general Klüke von Klugenau, who took Gotsatl and the important *a-ul* of Gherghebil, where the Kara Koisu and the Kasikumukh Koisu meet. Shamyl for the time being had to give up the thought of winning over the Avars, the strongest of all the mountain tribes in the Caucasus; but he made use of the time in making his power secure, and in binding together the followers of Muridism in the other parts of the land and in Chechnia, so as to strengthen the confederation against the Russians. These last made the so fateful mistake of bringing in the Kasimukhian Akhmed Khan from Mekhtuli, as provisional Khan of Avaria; he was the deadly foe of Hadji Murad, and by so doing they estranged the latter.

In March 1837 Shamyl succeeded in utterly destroying a Russian force near his headquarters at the *a-ul* of Ashilta on the Andian Koisu, near where it meets the Avarian Koisu. A fresh Russian army marched in in May under the command of General Feze; Ashilta was taken on the 9th of June and utterly destroyed, and so, too, a few days later the strong *a-ul* of Akhulgo near by.

But at this same time Shamyl was fighting the Russians at the strong *a-ul* of Tilitl in the mountains south of Khunsakh. Feze hastened thither to support his countrymen. With the help of their artillery the Russians succeeded in taking one-half of the *a-ul*, the other being held by Shamyl. But the Russians had now lost heavily and their position was a dangerous one. When Shamyl proposed an armistice, after some days' negotiations an agreement was reached, and on the 7th of July the Russians withdrew to Khunsakh. The Russians insisted that Shamyl and his chiefs[1] had submitted and sworn allegiance; but this is not borne out by two communications from Shamyl to General Feze, which, on the contrary, presuppose a truce on equal terms, even if Shamyl and his leaders gave three hostages. Nor is it borne out by the way the Russians withdrew along a route laid down by Shamyl, leaving the battlefield to the enemy.

Shamyl published a proclamation announcing a great victory over the Russians, who had been driven out of Daghestan; and many tribes that had fallen away now joined him again. When he came back to Ashilta he was kindled to a blazing wrath at the sight of his once so rich and flourishing *a-ul*, now a great blackened heap of ruins; not one of the five hundred houses was left standing; the mosque where he had been consecrated *imam* was levelled with the ground; the glorious fruit-gardens and vineyards had been laid waste, the vines torn up, the fruit trees cut down, the maize trampled

[1] A band of remarkable men. One of them was Kibit Mahoma, who had risen to be the ruler, kadi, of Tilitl by treacherously murdering the native begs and their families, thirty-three in all. He was one of Shamyl's chief supporters till nearly the end of the war in 1859, but then left him in the lurch and went over to the Russians.

underfoot, the water leads knocked down. This was
how the Russians behaved in a land where they
had forced a way in as foreigners, and where
they had no right but only might. He swore
vengeance.

He now chose as his headquarters the *a-ul* of
Akhulgo, which lay a little lower down on the right
bank of the Andian Koisu on two inaccessible
mountains; and he at once set to work to make
this natural fortress impregnable. As he had seen
that the strong stone towers of the mountain peoples
could not stand up under the fire of the Russian
guns, this remarkable commander dug himself into
the mountain with casemates.

Meanwhile it had been planned that the Tsar
Nicholas I should visit the Caucasus in the autumn
of 1837, and for the Russians it was highly important
to have Shamyl on friendly terms, and that he should
meet the Tsar in Tiflis. The brave and capable
General Klugenau was appointed to carry on the
negotiations, and there was a dramatic meeting
between him and Shamyl in a wild mountain gorge
near Ghimri on the 18th of September, 1837. Shamyl
came to the meeting with over two hundred armed
Murids on horseback in their brightly coloured garb
with turbans, while Klugenau had only an aide-
de-camp, fifteen Don Cossacks, and ten natives
with him. He applied every resource within the
range of his eloquence, but Shamyl was adamant.
When Klugenau saw it was hopeless, he rose and
held out his hand to take leave of Shamyl, but a
Murid rushed forward, held his arm, and said that

the leader of the faithful must not touch a giaour's
(unbeliever's) hand. The hot-tempered general
was furious, and raised the crutch he always
walked with to knock off the Murid's turban. Then,
luckily Shamyl grasped the crutch, held back the
Murid, who had drawn his *kindjal* (dagger), in a
thundering voice ordered his men to stay where they
were, and bade Klugenau go off without delay.
But the furious Austrian, utterly heedless of the
danger, gave free rein to his tongue, uttering the
most violent abuse against all mountaineers, until
his aide-de-camp succeeded in pulling him away
by the tip of his cloak, and at length prevailed on
him to go. He then slowly mounted his horse, and
walked away without deigning to glance at the
Murids. The future, as so often, was hanging by a
hair; if the blow with the crutch had not been held
up at the last moment by Shamyl, Klugenau and
all his men would undoubtedly have been slain;
while Shamyl and many of those nearest him would
probably have also been killed in the fight. The
war in the following years would have gone quite
otherwise, but perhaps the lives of many thousands
could have been spared. Tsar Nicholas soon after
made the journey to Transcaucasia, from September
till November, but he did not meet Shamyl.

Shamyl's power in Daghestan and Chechnia
grew steadily during 1838, and the Russians saw
that serious measures must be taken against him.
In May, General Grabbe marched out with an
army from Vnezapnaya against Akhulgo, hoping
to shut Shamyl in there, and finally settle accounts

with him. Shamyl came to meet him with a strong force by the inaccessible *a-ul* of Arguami to bar his way. But on the 30th of May and the 1st of June the *a-ul* was stormed, and as usual there was a bloody fight from street to street and house to house. The whole *a-ul* was plundered and laid in ruins, while Shamyl withdrew.

After much difficulty Grabbe stood with his army before Akhulgo on the 12th of June. Shamyl with 4,000 men, women, and children was now surrounded here, and of these 4,000 scarcely one-fourth were men fit to bear arms. But the fortress was too strong to be taken at once by storm; it had to be besieged, and the bombardment began. After about a month's siege the storm was attempted on the 16th of July; but the Russians were beaten back with heavy losses, and the siege was renewed in the hope of starving the enemy out, while the fortress was bombarded unceasingly the whole time by the Russian artillery. Conditions inside grew steadily worse; on the 27th of July parleys were at last opened, and the batteries ceased fire for a few hours. But there was no result, as Grabbe's essential condition was that Shamyl must submit to Russian supremacy, and as earnest of his good will send his son Jamalu'd-din as hostage. Firing was renewed. On the 12th of August Shamyl himself sent an envoy, and firing again was stopped for some hours. This time again there was no result; there was a parley, but it was soon evident that he only wanted to gain time to strengthen his works. On the 16th of August an ultimatum was sent him that unless his

son was handed over before night-time Akhulgo
would be stormed next morning.

As Jamalu'd-din did not come, the storm began
on the morning of the 17th of August, and this time
the preparations were better. The attackers, it is
true, suffered heavy losses, but progress was made
and in Shamyl's ranks many of his best men fell.
As further resistance looked hopeless, he at length
yielded, hoisted the white flag, and with a heavy
heart sent his beloved son of twelve years to the
hated foe. For the next three days there were
negotiations for the surrender of Akhulgo, but
Shamyl's conditions could not be accepted, and
on the 21st of August the storm was renewed. On
the first day little progress was made, but on the
morning after at dawn it started again. There was
dreadful house-to-house fighting. At last Akhulgo
was taken, but the fighting went on a week longer
in the half-underground stone houses and in the
caves where the mountaineers had entrenched
themselves and refused to yield; even women and
children with *kindjals* and stones in their hands threw
themselves against the bayonets or leaped into the
abyss; mothers killed their children that they might
not fall into the hands of the hated Russians. The
fight was a terrible one.

The siege lasting seventy days was at an end;
but where was Shamyl, the main actor in the
drama? Search was made high and low, in every
hole and corner; all the bodies were examined;
but he could not be found among either the dead
or the living. The fortress had been cut off on every

side; as at Ghimri, he had disappeared in an inexplicable way. This still further added to the belief in his holiness; it was said that Mohammed himself had come down to rescue him.

Later it became known that in the night of the 21st of August, with a wife and child and a few faithful companions, he had taken refuge in one of the caves in the face of the mountain above the Koisu. Next night they climbed down to the river, crept along down its bank, and in the darkness came upon a guard; there was a fight and Shamyl and his little son on his mother's back were wounded; but the lieutenant of the guard was killed, and so they got through the Russian lines.

The Russians were elated with their victory; Shamyl's power was now finally broken; he was a poor, homeless, wounded fugitive, bereft of everything and without followers. But before a year had gone by this lonely fugitive was standing again at the head of a people in arms. While the plundering and wasting by the Russians was but firing the hate of the mountain tribes, Shamyl made his way to Chechnia, where the terribly cruel government of the Russian general Pullo had exasperated those Chechens who had submitted to the Russians. They flocked now round Shamyl, and by March 1840 war was once more in full swing. Shamyl, having won fame as a commander in the treeless mountain valleys of Daghestan, quickly showed himself to be a master also in the fighting in the thick forests of Chechnia. He soon extended his activities to Daghestan also, where his old followers came pouring in together under his flag.

In November of that year something happened that was to have fateful results for the Russians. Hadji Murad, who all along had been their friend and ally, had had the suspicion brought on him by his enemy Akhmed Khan of Mekhtuli—provisional ruler of Avaria—of being in secret correspondence with Shamyl. He was arrested and taken to the Russian headquarters under a strong escort. On a narrow path along the mountain-side, where they had to go in single file, he suddenly jerked away the ropes holding him and jumped over the cliff. All thought it was certain death, but he escaped with a broken leg, and, although badly hurt, he managed to drag himself to friends, and from now on became the dangerous foe of the Russians. He joined Shamyl, who appointed him *naib*, and gradually he won the Avars over to his side.

Shamyl chose the *a-ul* of Dargo in Chechnia (Ichkeria) as his capital, and during the following years used his time in organizing his kingdom. He divided it into districts governed by *naibs*, each of whom had to furnish at least three hundred mounted fighting-men. The core of a standing army was formed from these mounted men, chosen from every tenth farmstead, and quartered in each *a-ul*, which had to keep their horses, till their land, and reap their crops. These men had always to be ready to carry out orders, and when a campaign was over they came back to their *a-uls*, where they also kept a hold on the other inhabitants. If needful their strength could be raised by the addition of a man from each farmstead. Furthermore, every man between fifteen and fifty was bound to enter the army if needed. Shamyl brought in systematic taxation, and strengthened his government through every means. In 1840, too, he founded orders for the reward of bravery. An express-post was set up to carry news and commands speedily throughout the land. On the whole he proved a great organizer, but he was terribly harsh and often cruel; he was followed by his executioner carrying a heavy long-handled axe and ready to cut off hands and heads at once, if there was the least suspicion of untrustworthiness. Thus Shamyl's sway was feared, but not loved, especially in Avaria, where moreover he had had a share in the murder of the Khans; this was never forgotten.

In 1841 the Russians again attacked, but with little success; Shamyl and his horsemen made most daring raids into their territory where they least expected him; he even penetrated into the land of the Kumyks as far as the town and fort of Kizliar in the north on the lower Terek, and with a rich booty, many prisoners, and great flocks of horned cattle he made his way home again right between two Russian divisions.

At the end of May 1842, while Shamyl was on an expedition against the Kasimukhians in southern Daghestan, General Grabbe with an army of 10,000 men and twenty-four guns marched into Chechnia to take Dargo. On the road, however, bands of the inhabitants swarmed round him, attacking first from one side, then from another; after three unfortunate days Grabbe had to abandon the undertaking, and the army marched back in a sorry plight, and having lost heavily. At the end of June, Grabbe once more attacked, this time in northern Daghestan; but he had no greater success. Once more he had to withdraw with heavy losses, and was forced to give up any further attempt.

In the summer of 1843 Shamyl felt himself strong enough for a more extensive campaign against the Russians in Daghestan. Suddenly, on the 27th of August, he set out with an army from his quarters at Dilim in Chechnia; in less than twenty-four hours he was standing in front of the *a-ul* of Untsukul in Avaria, sixty kilometres to the south, and here he was met on the same day by Kibit Mahoma from Tilitl and Hadji Murad from Avaria with strong forces; there were now 10,000 men gathered together. The speed and precision with which the long marches were carried out by the large bodies of cavalry right under the eyes of the Russian general, and the accuracy with which the several divisions operated together, show the high capacity of Shamyl as an army leader.

Untsukul had openly deserted his side, and furthermore had received a Russian garrison. It was of the greatest importance to show that such a thing could not be done with impunity. Some Russian companies, 500 men in all with two guns, that heedlessly hastened to the relief from Ghimri near by, were wholly wiped out, only a few men escaping. Untsukul was taken by storm, and the garrison in the Russian fort surrendered after so brave a resistance that Shamyl, to show his respect, let the commander, Lieutenant Anozov, keep his sword.

Within twenty-five days (the 27th of August to the 21st of September) after his sudden appearance before Untsukul, Shamyl had taken all the Russian fortified places in Avaria except Khunsakh, the capital. He now went back to Dilim, and, after an unsuccessful attempt to take the fortress of Vnezapnaya to the north, he sent his men back to their homes. But suddenly, at the end of October, he marched once more to the attack. The important Russian fortress of Gherghebil on the southern border of Avaria was stormed on the 8th of November; out of the garrison only two officers and a few men were left alive (according to Gurko's report). On the 11th of November Shamyl surrounded the Russian commander-in-chief himself, General Gurko, in his headquarters at Temir-Khan-Shura; Khunsakh was abandoned by the Russians, but they were surrounded on the march at Ziriani on the 17th of November; and thus all the Russian forces in northern Daghestan were now shut up in four forts. Gurko was relieved by General Freitag, and the other detachments were also rescued; but by the end of November all the Russian troops had been driven out of northern Daghestan. Shamyl was master of the situation, and was stronger than ever before. The Russian losses since the 27th of August were 92 officers, 2,528 men, 12 fortified places, and 27 guns.

THE TOWN OF TEMIR-KHAN-SHURA, THE RUSSIAN HEADQUARTERS IN DAGHESTAN DURING THE WAR

RUINS OF GUNIB *A-UL* AND THE BIRCH-WOOD WHERE SHAMYI
SURRENDERED

THE CASTLE AND WALL AT DERBENT

An episode from this time gives a remarkable insight into Shamyl's character and his methods with his people. During the fighting in Daghestan he had not been able properly to defend Chechnia, and the Chechens on the lower slopes of the mountains and the plains to the north had suffered more than usually from the destruction wrought by the Russian invasion. In despair they sent four messengers to Shamyl at Dargo, begging either for adequate protection or for leave to make peace with the Russians. As the messengers, fearing for their lives, did not dare to go to the fanatical *imam* himself, by using intermediaries and making large gifts of money they prevailed on his old mother to speak on their behalf with her son, who greatly loved her; but he could not grant her request. He saw at once that to kill the messengers, send them back blinded, cut off their hands, or inflict some other mutilation (which would have been most like him) would entail incalculable consequences. He therefore made known the request of the Chechens, and announced that he was going to fast and pray in retirement until the Prophet himself should declare his will to him. He shut himself up within the mosque, while the Murids and inhabitants of Dargo gathered around it by his orders to join their prayers with his.

For three days and nights the door of the mosque stayed shut; the crowd without were worn from fasting and praying, and were worked up through the long wait into a state of religious fever. Then slowly the door opened and Shamyl was standing

on the threshold, pale and with bloodshot eyes
Accompanied by two Murids, he went up in silence
on to the flat roof of the mosque, and at his bidding
his mother was brought there, veiled in her white
shawl (chadra). Led by two mullahs, she drew
near her son with slow, faltering steps. For a few
minutes he gazed on her without speaking, then
lifted his eyes to Heaven, and called out:

"O great Prophet Mohammed! Holy are thy
commands and not to be altered! Let thy just
sentence be carried out as an example for all true
believers!"

Then, turning to the people, he told them that
the Chechens had forgotten their oath, and wished
to submit to the giaours. They had been shameless
enough to send men hither to Dargo to ask leave,
but as these men had not dared to come to him
himself, they had turned to his unhappy weak
mother, that she might speak on their behalf. Her
insistent representations and his boundless devotion
to her gave him boldness enough to ask God's
Prophet Mohammed himself what was his will.

"And look! Here with you around me, and
supported by your prayers, I have after three days'
fasting and praying been granted his gracious
answer to my presumptuous question. But this
answer has struck me like a thunderbolt. It is
Allah's will that the one who first told me about
the shameful purpose of the Chechen people shall
be punished with a hundred heavy lashes with the
whip, and this first one was—my own mother!"

At a sign from the *imam* the Murids tore the

chadra from the unhappy old woman, grasped her
by the hands, and began lashing her with a plaited
whip; a shudder of bewildered horror ran through
the crowd. At the fifth lash the victim swooned,
and Shamyl, beside himself with pain, stopped the
executioners and threw himself at his mother's feet.
The spectacle was heartrending, and with tears
and groans the onlookers begged for mercy for
their benefactress. In a few moments Shamyl rose
without a trace of his earlier emotion. Once more
he lifted his eyes to Heaven, and in a solemn voice
he called out: "There is only one God, and
Mohammed is His Prophet! O ye dwellers in Paradise, ye have listened to my fervent prayer, and
have allowed me to take on myself the rest of the
lashes that were awarded to my unhappy mother.
These lashes I most joyfully accept as a most
precious gift from your loving-kindness."

And with a smile on his lips he took off his red
cloak, and gave the two Murids heavy Nogai whips,
and told them that with his own hand he would
kill the man who should dare to be lenient in
carrying out the Prophet's will. In silence and
without the least sign of pain he took the remaining
ninety-five lashes. After putting on his cloak he
stepped down among the frightened crowd, and
asked: "Where are the scoundrels on whose account
my mother has had to suffer so ignominious a
punishment?" The wretched men were at once
dragged up and lay at his feet; their fate was
looked on as certain. But to their surprise and the
surprise of all he raised them up, saying: "Go back

to your people, and as the answer to your foolish prayer tell them all you have seen and heard."

What is probable is that in a scene such as this it is also the fanatical believer who takes part by the side of the mime; but we can easily understand that a masterly and dramatically planned performance such as this made a deep impression on the superstitious and credulous men of the mountains.

At this time Tsar Nicholas I was sitting in very ill humour in his palace in St. Petersburg, chafing angrily at the way things were going on in the Caucasus, and at the fact that this insolent bandit Shamyl was still quite free and able to oppose his, the all-powerful autocrat's, will. On the 18th of December, 1843, therefore, he gave his new commander-in-chief on this front, General Neidhardt, orders to force his way into the mountains and "strike at and scatter all Shamyl's hordes, destroy all his military works, take possession of all the most important points, and fortify those which it might seem essential to hold". So that all this might be carried out he gave orders for important additions to the strength of the army, more than doubling it. The plan was to be carried through unchanged, and to be brought to its completion by the end of 1844.

On the Russian side the greatest exertions were made with these increased numbers; but although their various attacks were partly successful, on the whole they failed, and yielded no lasting results; at the end of the year Shamyl's position and influence were just as strong.

In the summer one of those bloody deeds happened which, though they strengthened his authority at the moment, yet in the end helped to undermine it. One of his faithful friends had been killed near the *a-ul* of Tsonteri near Dargo as the result of a blood feud. Shamyl sent two hundred men to take some of the most important dwellers in the village for not having hindered the murder. This action of Shamyl was in utter contradiction with the generally received law (*adat*), under which blood revenge was actually a duty, although according to Shamyl's doctrine this was against the holy precepts (*sharvat*). The inhabitants therefore drove back the Murids by armed force. Then Shamyl came down upon the luckless *a-ul*, persuaded the inhabitants to yield, and every living soul, from the children to the oldest, was slain, in all a hundred families.

In the following years, in spite of the Tsar's orders and the strengthened forces, the Russians were no more successful. Although Shamyl could only put a fraction of such numbers in the field, and lacked artillery, but for such guns as he had taken, he was more than a match for them through the quick movements of his army of horsemen. He avoided fighting where the enemy could bring all his heavy forces into action and make full use of his artillery; but he did everything to draw them on farther and farther into the mountains and forests, and in the most difficult places he would fall by surprise on their rear or swarm all round them, make a violent attack, inflict heavy losses, and cut off or take their supplies; thus they could not carry out any important operations, and it would always end with their having once more to withdraw.

This was exactly what happened in Prince Vorontsov's disastrous campaign in 1845. Owing to his great reputation from the Napoleonic Wars, he had that year been appointed viceroy of the Caucacus and commander-in-chief. In obedience to the Tsar's orders he marched out on the 31st of May, 1845, from the fortress of Vnezapnaya in Chechnia with the finest army yet seen in the Caucasus, at least 18,000 strong. His objective was Shamyl's capital, Dargo. Without meeting any great direct resistance, but with heavy losses in that difficult country, he reached it on the 6th of July with a half-starved army in a bad condition, only to find the town burned down and laid waste by Shamyl, all supplies carried away, and no possibility of finding food, while his own convoys were in great part cut off with heavy losses. In the underground prisons in the town Shamyl had held thirty-three Russian officers and men; the Russians had hoped to rescue them, but Shamyl had had them all murdered.

Vorontsov's position was a serious one; he had now to try and bring back his army in safety with the utmost speed: it had shrunk down to 5,000 fit men, had to transport 1,100 wounded, and had food for only a few days. On the 13th of July the mournful retreat began under constant fighting and great obstacles. The losses were heavy: in four

days they were over 1,000 men, and the number
of wounded had grown to more than 2,000. Progress on the average was only 6½ kilometres daily.
Vorontsov on the 16th of July saw that it was
impossible to march any longer. They had to
encamp and await the relief, for which he had sent
several messengers, not knowing whether these
had got through. The 17th went by; the men had
nothing more to eat than a little maize they had
found in the fields around; the camp was ringed
round by Shamyl's men, and was being bombarded
by the guns he had taken. The 18th went by;
hunger began to gnaw; there was no more ammuni-
tion for the guns, and the men had only about
fifty rounds each left. It looked as though the end
was drawing nigh. Then, as the sun was near its
setting, the far-off thunder was heard of guns, of
many guns. At once the whole camp was on its feet;
they were filled with joy—even the wounded and
sick forgot all their wretchedness. It was General
Freitag who had come. The messengers had
reached him in Grozny on the night of the 15th of
July, and he rode 160 kilometres in two days,
gathering up his troops on the way; and at nine
o'clock on the evening of the 18th of July his
advanced troops had reached the other force.

After measuring his strength against Freitag,
Shamyl withdrew, and upbraided his *naibs* for
having after all let the booty escape them. On the
20th of July the remnant of the proud army reached
safety in the *a-ul* of Gherzel in the lowlands, but
not without further losses in the rearguard. Thus

ended the wretched Dargo expedition of 1845. Tsar Nicholas now began to understand that Imperial orders from St. Petersburg were not enough to lay the bandit Shamyl's head at his feet. Shamyl's most daring deed at this time was his raid into Kabardia on the lowlands both sides of the Terek north and north-west of Vladikavkaz. The brave mountain tribes in the north-western Caucasus, who were also carrying on a stern struggle for their freedom, were separated from Chechnia by the fruitful Kabardia, which since 1822 had been in Russian hands. If Shamyl could only succeed in getting the war-like and numerous Kabardians to rise and join him, his fighting strength would be very considerably increased, and there would be an unbroken line of communication with the north-western Caucasus. The Russians would then have to face an unbroken front and a confederation more dangerous than at any time before. Shamyl, therefore, made great efforts by way of promises and threats to persuade the Kabardians to join their fellow-believers against the unbelievers; and last of all in 1845 he sent them a proclamation drawn up in the strongest words within the range of his fiery eloquence, ending as follows: "But if ye still will believe the specious promises of the red-haired Christian dogs rather than my warnings, then shall I fulfil the promise made you by Kasi-Mullah: like dark storm-clouds shall my armies march over your *a-uls* to compel you by force to do that which ye have refused to do by your own good will. My road shall be marked by blood, and in my wake shall be fear and destruction; for where the might of the word is not enough, there must the deed stand by it to help.—God's servant, the *imam* Shamyl."

In the middle of April 1846 Shamyl suddenly attacked Kabardia from Chechnia in great strength. His hope was that the Kabardians, who were discontented with the Russian rule, would rise when he came to support them. But the capable General Freitag had suspected what he was going to do, and had therefore gathered a force together; he now hotly pursued Shamyl so as to cut him off. The Kabardians did not dare to rise, and Shamyl, afraid to meet Freitag in open fight on the treeless lowland, had to flee back to his mountains, only a few hours ahead of the Russians. Although his plan had failed, yet this bold attempt increased his reputation among the mountain tribes, and his losses had been unimportant; but Freitag had saved Russia from a great peril. For the rest of the year Shamyl's men gave the Russians little peace. With never a stop there were constant fresh attacks and raids, and the daring of the Murids went so far as to bombard Grozny itself (24th of July), and the new fort of Vozdvizhensko to the south (17th of August). The Russians, however, managed to strengthen their lines by building two new and important forts on this front. In southern Daghestan Shamyl himself was defeated near Kuteshi in October, and the whole of the fruitful and thickly inhabited Darghi district had to submit once more to the Russians.

In June 1847 Vorontsov laid siege to Gherghebil, which had been strongly fortified by Shamyl; he tried to storm it, but was hurled back with heavy losses and had to give up his purpose. He consoled himself by taking in August the still more strongly fortified *a-ul* of Salti after seven weeks' siege, but the Russian losses were 2,000 dead and wounded. In July of next summer (1848) Gherghebil also was taken after twenty-three days' siege by an army of 10,000. But they could not hold the town, and had to retreat, followed by the Murids, so that nothing was gained. In September 1848 the fort of Akhti, on the Samur river near the southern boundary of Daghestan, was attacked by Shamyl in great strength; it was, however, heroically defended by Colonel Roth and 500 men for over a week. Half the garrison was killed or wounded, the main powder-magazine had blown up, the walls were breached, the water used up, no food could be cooked. Shamyl had promised Roth's young daughter to the *naib* that should first plant his banner on the wall; but she and the soldiers' wives were resolved to blow themselves up rather than fall into the enemy's hands. When all hope had been given up a Russian force came at length to the relief.

In the following years there were no movements in the field of any importance; both the Russians and Shamyl mostly kept on the defensive, and on neither side were there any defeats or losses of importance. Taught by his dearly bought experience Vorontsov had gradually come to see more and more that neither Daghestan nor Chechnia could be taken by isolated campaigns, and that Shamyl's power could not be broken at one blow. There must be patient, methodical work to strengthen the Russian lines along the outermost boundaries, and to fortify them with a chain of strong forts linked by roads, and by building permanent quarters with adequate barracks; so gradually they would push these fortified lines forward. Together with this an attempt was made to cut down and thin out the forests in Chechnia, which gave the foe so great an advantage, and to make broad open roads through them, while the *a-uls* there were destroyed so far as might be.

Shamyl on his side made use of the time to establish his power firmly over the mountain tribes, and in 1849 it was at its height; but it was a pure despotism, and rested more and more on the executioner's axe. None dared oppose his will, not even the kinsmen of his victims. Thousands were always ready to sacrifice their lives at his bidding, and his chieftains were ready to lead them. First among these was Hadji Murad. He made raid after raid, each bolder than the last, into the heart of the enemy's country. There was no limit to his daring, and with his unrivalled resourcefulness and swiftness he always got away unharmed. In December 1846 he made his way with 500 men by night into Djengutai, the capital of Mekh-tuli, and carried off the widow of his old foe, Akhmed Khan, right under the nose of the strong Russian garrison. In April 1849 he surpassed his reputatation as the boldest of all the Murid leaders by a night raid on Temir-Khan-Shura itself, the military centre and capital of Russian Daghestan. This time he turned the shoes round on the horses to mislead his pursuers. On the 1st of July, 1851, with 500 horsemen he fell by night on the rich *a-ul* of Buïnakh, near the coast between Derbent and Petrovsk, killed Shakh Vali, brother of the *shamkhal* of Tarku, on his own threshold, and carried off captives his wife and children, for whom Shamyl afterwards got a heavy sum as ransom. On this occasion Hadji Murad with his men rode 150 kilometres in less than thirty hours, and escaped without any losses, although they were hotly pursued. His deeds of daring were manifold, and he was the terror of all his foes around.

But he was slandered and made an object of suspicion to Shamyl, who was envious of his renown, and afraid of him because of the murder of the Khans of Khunsakh. Shamyl resolved therefore to be rid of this man, whose popularity might become dangerous; and at a secret meeting at Avturi in Chechnia, Hadji Murad was condemned to death. Being warned at the last moment, he fled in November 1851 to the Russian fort of Vozdvizhensko, hoping with the help of the Russians to take revenge on Shamyl. The Russians were greatly elated at this new acquisition, and believed it to be the beginning of desertions from Shamyl. Hadji Murad was granted leave to stay, under a constant watch, at several Russian military posts near the boundary, where he might be in touch

ASTRAKHAN: THE TOWER OVER THE ENTRANCE TO THE KREMLIN WITH THE CATHEDRAL ON THE LEFT AND THE RUINS OF THE BAZAAR IN THE FOREGROUND ON THE RIGHT

FISHING-BOATS AT THE WHARF BEFORE THE FREEZING-WORKS

GOOD-BYE TO MAKHACH KALA

LIGHTERS BEING TOWED UP THE VOLGA IN THE DELTA

VILLAGE IN THE DELTA ON THE RIGHT BANK OF THE VOLGA

THE LOW LAND WITH ARMS OF THE RIVER ON THE LEFT BANK
OF THE VOLGA

with his friends in Daghestan. He hoped for a
favourable opportunity to strike a blow with
Russian help at Shamyl with his accustomed daring.
Meanwhile Shamyl was holding his family prisoners,
and threatening to dishonour the women and kill
or put out the eyes of his beloved son Yusuf. They
had first to be set free by an exchange of prisoners
before he could do anything. But at last, wearied
of waiting for the Russian promises to be fulfilled,
and tormented by inaction and anxiety for his
family, he fled in April 1852 with his five companions to get back once more to his mountains.
Before they could get through the Russian lines
they were surrounded by a great number of pursuers; a fight of one against a hundred was hopeless,
but they had no thought of surrendering; they
only entrenched themselves, intoned their death-
song, and fired. As long as they had cartridges they
kept the foe at bay. Hadji Murad was hit by a
bullet, put a wad in the wound and went on firing;
then he was mortally wounded, but still kept up a
fire. He then crept out, stood on his feet, and rushed
on them with his *kindjal* (dagger), till he fell pierced
by several bullets.

Hotly thou camest, O death-bearing ball that I spurned,
 For thou wast my slave.
And thou, black earth, that my battle steed trampled and
 churned,
 Wilt cover my grave.
Cold art thou, O Death, yet I was thy Lord and Master.
My body sinks fast to earth; my soul to Heaven flies faster.[1]

---

[1] From a Chechen death-song; English translation by J. F.
Baddeley, *op. cit.*, p. 489.

Two of his brave men fell in the fight, three were taken prisoners and executed. This was on the 24th of April, 1852. The Russians had lost one of their most dreaded opponents, but his name will live long in the mountain valleys he so heroically defended.

It might have been expected that Shamyl, during the Crimean War from 1853–6, would have used the opportunity in alliance with the Turks and the Western Powers to aim smashing blows against the Russian dominion in the Caucasus. But, exasperated by the extraordinarily foolish policy of the Turks, Shamyl broke off all relations with them; and as the Western Powers, too, had not understood their great possibilities on this front, Shamyl lay quiet throughout most of the war, giving up his time to keeping his hold over the people, who were beginning to grow weary, and were worn out by the never-ending warfare.

In 1854 he invaded Georgia, and plundered the fruitful Alazán valley; his troops were then beaten, but a party got as far as the castle of Tsinondal, and took prisoners the two Georgian princesses, the sisters Chavchavadze and Orbeliani. When they were ransomed later, Shamyl, besides receiving a sum of money, was at last able to get back his son Jamalu'd-din, whom in 1839 he had had to give up at Akhulgo. But after fifteen years' education in Russia—from the age of twelve—where he had become an officer in the army, he was utterly estranged from his father, his people, and his land. This was a bitter disappointment to the father;

the son pined away, grew melancholy, and in three years was dead.

When peace had been made in Paris on the 30th of March, 1856, Russia could again set about the conquest of the Caucasus in earnest, and this time in even greater strength. Prince Baryatinsky was made commander-in-chief and viceroy in the Caucasus (22nd of July, 1856). For Shamyl's people the rest had not been long enough to heal the deep wounds of war; there was not a family but had lost men. They were war-weary; and during the time of inaction there was no shining deed of arms, no great victory over the foe, to stir their lives anew. Moreover, the people were murmuring louder and louder at Shamyl's tyrannical rule and his cruelty, which made themselves especially felt in peace-time. Many, therefore, were quite ready to go over to the Russians, if only they could trust to their protecting them against the mighty and much-feared *imam*; and, curiously enough, the Crimean War had very greatly increased the mountain peoples' respect for the power of Russia. An empire which had been able to stand up against mighty Turkey and the still mightier Western Powers without being destroyed, was one which it was hopeless for them to fight against, while on the other hand it could defend them. Thus many fell away one by one from Shamyl and went over to the Russians. His attempt to come to an understanding with the tribes in the north-west Caucasus came to naught.

While the Russians all the time could be sending

fresh or strengthened forces against him, he ha
but his one army, always the same, and his Murids
who were ever being thinned through losses and
desertions. There was, moreover, the fact that the
new Russian firearms and rifles were far better
than those of the mountain peoples. The Russian
lines were pushed on farther and farther round
Shamyl, who after the destruction of Dargo in 1845
had chosen Veden in Chechnia as his headquarters. On the 1st of April, 1859, this strong
fortress was taken by storm by the "three-eyed"
General Yevdokimov after two months' siege,
with remarkably small losses for the Russians.
Shamyl now went off into Daghestan, and with iron
courage strove to put up a defence there in permanent positions. But more and more of the
mountain tribes now fell away from him; his most
faithful chieftains failed him; even Kibit Mahoma,
the fanatical kadi of Tilitl, went over to the Russians
and stood opposed to him. Betrayed and forsaken,
with wives and children and a small following he
now took refuge for the last time on the mountain
known as Gunib, on the left bank of the Kara
Koisu, where they were still faithful to him. This
was in August, and a few days later, on the 9th,
the Russian army came up and the siege began.

The mountain is like a huge truncated three-
sided pyramid, whose sides rise perpendicularly
over the mountain land around. The flat top is perhaps ten square kilometres in area, with grazing
and plough-land, birch-woods and brooks running
through it. On this plain lies the *a-ul* of Gunib;

and here were several farmsteads and mills, and other sources of supplies. With the men of the *a-ul* and his small following he had altogether about four hundred men.

This natural stronghold Shamyl sought by every means to strengthen. Had it been defended by proper numbers the mountain would not have been easy to take, but his four hundred men with only four guns, needless to say, were not enough to defend so much ground against the greatly superior forces that soon surrounded the mountain on every side. Prince Baryatinsky himself came there. Negotiations were started, and Shamyl was called upon to surrender on honourable terms, which he refused; he could not give up the cause he had fought for his whole life long.

After two weeks' siege and various feigned attacks on the eastern and easiest accessible side, the Russians advanced to the storm on the night 24th–25th of August (5th–6th of September). As day broke, several battalions by help of ladders and ropes climbed up on the north and south sides, where the mountain people believed no one could do so. They did not succeed in taking the defenders wholly by surprise, who threw themselves on the Russians; but Russian troops made their appearance on the south-eastern side at the time. After putting up a hot defence with heavy losses, the defenders fled into the *a-ul*, where Shamyl shut himself in with his family. About a hundred Murids who had thus escaped fell on the attackers with sabres and *kindjals* (daggers), but were killed to a man.

Prince Baryatinsky wished to take Shamyl alive, if possible; the Russians therefore made a halt before the *a-ul*, which soon was encircled by fourteen battalions. As parliamentary, an Armenian colonel, was sent to Shamyl. The old fanatic wavered; had he been alone, he would probably have fought on to the death; but could he sacrifice his wives and children? This was to touch him at his tenderest spot. He mounted and rode out of the *a-ul*, but he had not come far before the Russian soldiers, seeing their thirty years' foe at last in their hands, gave a loud cheer. Shamyl grew pale, pulled up his horse, and turned back towards the *a-ul*. Then the ready-witted Armenian ran after him, and called out that the cheers were a token of esteem towards him. Followed by about fifty Murids, the last remnants of his once so powerful army, he then rode to the little birch-wood near, where Prince Baryatinsky surrounded by his staff received him, and he surrendered himself with his Murids.

Thus ended Shamyl's long fight against the penetration of his mountain world by foreign unbelievers, and against their conquest of its peoples. When as a prisoner he journeyed through Russia to St. Petersburg, he was deeply struck by the size of the towns—so huge, compared with his small *a-uls*—the many people and the vast stretches of the land; and he was dismayed to think that it was against this mighty empire that he with his small forces had fought for over thirty years. He was hailed on his journey by the Russians as a great hero, and Tsar Alexander II received him near Kharkov, and clasped and kissed him as a friend. Shamyl, who had feared retaliation for the cruelty he had so often shown towards Russian prisoners, was deeply touched, and was overwhelmed with gratitude for this magnanimity. In the evening a great ball was given for him; but when he and his Murids saw the ladies' dresses and the way they exposed themselves, they were dismayed, turned away, and started praying. That gentlemen and ladies should embrace one another before everyone and dance together was beyond their understanding.

He was assigned the little town of Kaluga, southwest of Moscow, as his abode. A good and roomy house was built there for him and his family—three wives and sons and daughters—and the Tsar granted him a yearly pension of 10,000 silver roubles. Shamyl was deeply grateful for the kindness shown him. In 1870 he was granted leave to make the pilgrimage to Mecca; from there he went to Medina, dying here in 1871, seventy-four years old.

When Shamyl had been taken prisoner there was none left who could gather the Lesghis and Chechens to fight the Russians, and the whole of Daghestan and Chechnia made its submission. The Russian forces were thereby set free on this front, and could now be concentrated against the north-western Caucasus, where the Abkhasians and the Circassian or Cherkess tribes (the Adigheb) were still defending themselves with the utmost heroism.

Shamyl had often tried to get these tribes to join him and his cause. His difficulty was that his own area, Daghestan and Chechnia, was separated from these north-western tribes by the Christian Ossetes, Khevsurs, Pshavs, and other Georgian mountain tribes, who had joined the Russians, or anyhow were not on hostile terms with them. Moreover, the Abkhasians, too, were in great part Christians. As early as 1842 he had sent a *naib*, Hadji Mehmet, to them, who had considerable success, but died in 1844, possibly poisoned. In the same year Shamyl sent a new *naib*, Hadji Soliman, who was bolder and more insistent, winning many over to Islam and Shamyl's doctrine, and preaching the Holy War. Then in 1846 there came a young man, Mohammed Emin, from Shamyl, who had been his first writer and secretary; he was to win great influence. Almost at once Hadji Soliman disappeared in a mysterious way—he was probably murdered—and the young Mohammed Emin soon succeeded by his shrewd and moderate ways in strengthening and widening his power over large parts of the land. In no little degree he did this by supporting the people everywhere against the nobles and princes; and he did away with the very many heavy forced calls on the freemen, and set free a great number of slave families and thralls. Bit by bit he won over most of the land, and brought many of its dwellers over to Islam. He divided the country up into districts, and organized it in a masterly way so as for the first time to act and fight as a body. He was a worthy disciple of Shamyl, and for the Russians a dangerous foe; but it could never come to any effective co-operation with

Shamyl owing to the distance that lay between them. Moreover, on the one hand the aristocratic Circassians with their nobility and princes had no liking for the democratism of Shamyl and his mountain tribes, and were afraid of him for the cruelty with which he had slain and rooted out the princes in Daghestan; while, on the other hand, the Christian part of the people had no wish to join this fanatical Mussulman and his holy war against the Christians.

Then came the Crimean War in 1853, and it might have been thought that the time had come for the Abkhasians and Circassians, with the support of the Turks and the Western Allied Powers, utterly to destroy the Russians in their own part of the Caucasus. But owing to the very clumsy policy of the Turks the opposite thing happened: the Turks declared Abkhasia and Circassia to be Turkish provinces, thereby stirring up against themselves the mountain peoples, who were, and meant to be, independent. Furthermore, the Sultan and the Porte mistrusted Mohammed Emin and Shamyl, who, they believed, wished to rule the Caucasus themselves and had no intention of submitting to Turkish dominion. Instead of using Mohammed Emin as a powerful ally, and stirring up the whole land to fight, all they succeeded in doing through their many intrigues against him was to weaken his power and split up the land he had organized. The result was that the mountaineers kept quiet during the war, and thereby unwillingly helped the Russians.

As soon as peace had been made, the Russians were able from 1856 to attack the Caucasus peoples with all their strength. As we said above, after Shamyl had been overcome they had been able to concentrate their forces against the Circassians and Abkhasians, whose great weakness was that their many tribes never felt themselves to be united as a national whole, and could never combine for any length of time against the common foe. The improvement in the Russian firearms, moreover, gave them a great advantage against the mountain peoples. These heroic peoples, however, defended themselves for another five years, until at length they had to yield in 1864, after a fight for freedom that had lasted, with breaks, for nearly a century. But so strong was the urge towards freedom of the Circassians that nearly 400,000 of them, together with some of the Abkhasians and Chechens, left their beloved mountain valleys and migrated to Turkey rather than bow their heads under the Russian yoke. The lot of many of them was a hard one: so bad were the arrangements to receive them in Turkish Asia that many sank altogether under through want; some did settle, but others became dreaded bands of robbers in the mountains there.

Even before the 1917 revolutions there had been a Socialist movement among the peoples in Daghestan, and when the February revolution of 1917 came, they at once joined in. Kerensky sent new representatives there, but now a Communist movement against him was started, led by Makhach

Dakhadayev. On the other hand, there was a strong anti-revolutionary Mohammedan movement under the *imam* Gochinsky, the most important man in the religious body, and one who had great influence in the Avar and Andi districts. At first he worked with Kerensky, but soon broke off all relations with him and stood opposed to Russia. In September 1917 he was fighting together with his followers against the Russians, and his commander, Uzun Hadji, quickly captured the Avar, Andi, and Chechen territories.

During the Bolshevist October revolution Daghestan was separated from Bolshevist Russia by the Don and the Kuban districts, which were anti-revolutionary, and Gochinsky was then the strongest man there. He declared *ghazavat* (the holy war) against Armenia, and also sent his forces against Baku. But at that time the power in Baku had come into the Bolshevists' hands, and they drove Gochinsky's army back. The Red army of the Soviet government also took Petrovsk and Shura. In August 1918 Petrovsk was taken by the adventurer Bicherakhov, supported by the British. The position of the Soviet Government in Shura was then a difficult one, threatened as it was by him from the south, by Gochinsky's Chechen bands on the other side, and from Azerbaidjan by the Turkish army, which took Baku in September.

In November 1918 the Turkish army defeated Bicherakhov, and took Petrovsk and Shura. A new so-called democratic (Menshevist) government was then set up in Daghestan, to which Gochinsky also gave his adherence, and joined it as a member. When the armistice was concluded in December 1918, the Turks marched away; the British army came from Persia to Daghestan, and supported Denikin, who sent a part of his army there. Uzun Hadji fought against him, but Gochinsky refused to move against the White Russians.

In June 1919 Denikin was very strong in Daghestan, and officially Gochinsky was working along with him. Uzun Hadji, however, who had become Emir of North Caucasia under the protectorate of the Sultan of Turkey, became estranged from Gochinsky, and went on fighting against Denikin. Then the Turks under Nuri Pasha came to Azerbaidjan, and afterwards to Daghestan; they fought both Denikin and the Red army. This last steadily grew stronger, and as in the spring of 1920 it was having success on the north, Nuri Pasha sought to join forces with Denikin. He was unsuccessful, however, and withdrew. Meanwhile Uzun Hadji died, and his monarchy came to an end. The White army also left Petrovsk and marched to Baku, and the Red army took the whole of Daghestan. Then the Autonomous Soviet-Socialist Republic (A.S.S.R.) of Daghestan was set up with internal self-government.

Chechnia became an Autonomous District, as also did Kabardia, and the Districts of the Adhigeb and the Circassians; to a certain extent they have internal self-government. Abkhasia became a Soviet-Socialist Republic (S.S.R.) united with Georgia.

VIII

EXCURSIONS IN DAGHESTAN

VIII

EXCURSIONS IN DAGHESTAN

We had now finished with the museum (p. 113 f.), and after this flight into the dead and gone romance of these mountain valleys, we were brought back with a jolt to everyday life, as from the cool museum we stepped out into the burning sun to drive to the cotton-mill. It is one of the most important industrial undertakings here; and seemed to be working very well, with skilled workmen. Each day 20,000 *arshin* (= 14,224 metres) of cotton-stuff are woven, and this is made in part from cotton grown in Daghestan. When the mill was built in 1921 without any subvention from Moscow, it had 700 workers. In 1924 their number was 560. Among the other industrial undertakings in this town special mention may be made of a factory for preserving the wonderful Daghestan fruit. We were given many samples of its products, which are exported; they were extraordinarily good, and will undoubtedly find a wide market. Then we drove up to the great reservoir with the new canal, which brings water from the stream running down from the mountains a little west of the town. From this reservoir the town now gets its drinking-water, which is cleaned in a great filter. But the canal brings so much that a great part of it can be used for irrigation.

Makhach Kalá lies on a plain which runs back from four to ten kilometres from the shore up to the foot of the steep mountain slopes. To the north it spreads out wide in the low-lying swampy land about the Terek. To the south it runs with a varying breadth between the coast and the eastern slope of the Caucasus to its narrowest part at the town of Derbent, which for centuries was the gate from the south to this northern world. Farther south again it slightly widens towards Baku with its wonderful oil-fields.

As I was standing after lunch in the passage at the top of the stairs in the President's house, a child came tottering along the passage. I was quite spellbound—an angel of God cut straight out of a picture by Correggio—I had not thought that we had such beings from Heaven in the house. It was Korkmazov's son, who lived there alongside us on the same floor, and the boy had come to look for his father. Then the overwhelming joy when he came, and the boy sprang into his arms—it was an irresistible sight.

In the afternoon I went for a walk along the shore where there was a crowd of naked boys and men bathing. They all kept in the green water, where they paddled about, dipped, and swam a little; but none swam out into the deep water. All seemed to be living God's joyous days to the full. Only here and there a few groups of small girls and young women could be seen bathing, but they kept far away from the others, and but few women met the eye anywhere.

When I heard that in the west of the plain there were great swarms of locusts that were wholly destroying the fields, I wished very much to see this; and Quisling and I were then given the choice in the afternoon between either driving out there or going to see the remarkable sulphur baths at Talgi on the plain to the south. We chose the locusts, and motored north-west along beside the railway over a rather uneven road, and were well shaken up. The Commissary for agriculture went with us, a young and wide-awake man, with a remarkable likeness to Charles XII of Sweden.

We drove on a long time, but saw no locusts, and the fields lay fruitful and green with no sign of any blight. But when we had gone about twenty kilometres, far away in front of us towards the setting sun it looked as though a mist was lying on the fields. It spread out more and more as we went on, grew higher and thicker. When we came up to it, it turned out to be made up wholly by thick swarms of locusts, that now towards evening were settling and not flying so high in the air as earlier in the day. But how unbelievably many of them there were! When one of our men fired his rifle over the maize-fields, the swarms rose up like dark, billowy clouds, and one understood how they can cover the sky in dense masses and darken the sun. And it was the same over the maize-fields in every direction—a distressing and hopeless sight. The leaves were all eaten off every maize-plant; the bare stalks showed starkly everywhere. The people were utterly powerless against a plague of this kind, and had to look on helplessly while the whole of their crop was eaten up and destroyed. They said that something can be done by sprinkling sulphur, and that aeroplanes have been used for this purpose with good results: but it is doubtful whether anything can really help.

These swarms of locusts are carried by the wind, and generally come from uncultivated land, where the eggs can be laid and hatched out without disturbance. The only practical method, therefore, is to attack them there before they grow to maturity, and destroy their eggs and lavae by burning off the ground and sprinkling petroleum over it.

North of the mountains in northern Persia, towards the Caspian south of Azerbaidjan, there is said to be a lot of uncultivated land of this kind where the locust swarms are formed. The Persians themselves are little interested in destroying them, since the wind seldom carries them southwards over the high mountain ranges; while they are often spread northwards over Azerbaidjan and Daghestan. By agreement with the Persians the Transcaucasian government of late years has used destructive methods on the ground in spring in these Persian districts, and in this way the plague has been greatly lessened. But the swarms we saw here had certainly not come all that way from Persia; they came from places nearer. Where they now were the whole crop would be destroyed; luckily, the area so far was not very great, but the question was where the wind would carry them.

These locusts are rather large and of a brownish colour, five or six centimetres long. It is a pity they cannot be used as food instead of the corn they destroy; but so far as I could find out they are not

eaten by the people in these districts, though they
are roasted and eaten in great quantities by the
Arabs. It was but small consolation to see a load of
hay being driven home over this ravaged plain;
the hay had probably been cut before the locusts
came. But twilight was falling, and we had to go
home. It was a remarkable sight to see how sharply
marked off was the tract where the swarms were:
a short way off the maize-fields were still standing
green and unharmed. But against the darkening
sky here and there we could see locusts whirring
along before the light wind, perhaps forerunners of
what was to come. This would depend on the way
the wind should blow in the next days.

Our kind hosts wished very much to show us the
various aspects of their remarkable country, and
they were particularly bent on our having a good
impression of all its sources of wealth and possibilities
for the future. There were the oil-fields on the
southern plain, and the fisheries, and the great
openings for agricultural development, sulphur and
mineral deposits, and much besides.

Early next morning (Wednesday, the 8th of
July) the two Presidents, Quisling, and I went by
train along the coast southwards over the lowlands.
In the same train was a band of young students of
both sexes from the University of Kharkov in the
Ukraine, who were travelling to study the Caucasus.
At a station where we made a stop they came in a
ceremonious deputation, and a speech was made in
German expressing their gratitude to me for having
helped to relieve the distress in the Ukraine during

and after the great famine of 1921–2. On that occasion I had sent Captain Quisling as my representative to Kharkov to organize and direct our work. Later, too, the international organization for helping students had in co-operation with me established places for meals in Kharkov, where the many needy students were given their frugal daily fare.

They were most attractive young women and men, radiating light-heartedness, health, and strength; they were bound to have a splendid trip, and to learn much from it.

At a station farther on we alighted and the train went on with its load of youthful good spirits on its way to the south, and from the windows their hands waved good-bye.

We were met by a big mounted escort; the men had come from near and far on their fairly small but good horses. Several carriages and a motor-car were awaiting us. Samursky, Korkmazov, and I drove together in a light carriage over the plain, surrounded by many mounted men in front, at our sides, and behind. It was not long before Samursky also had to take a horse and gallop with them. The endurance of these small horses was remarkable. Quisling, who was driving in the car, told me that many of the horsemen galloped the whole way ahead of it, although it drove quite fast.

We came to some oil-wells which the Nobel Company had formerly tried to work. There were several towers with borings from that time, and we saw oil and water flowing out together from

SMALL SQUARE WITH FOUNTAIN AT TARKI

THE HIGHEST PART OF TARKI

AN AIRY SLEEPING-PLACE

BUFFALOES IN THE WATER
"THE BUFFALOES LAY AS DEEP IN THE WATER-HOLES AS THEY COULD'

them. There was undoubtedly a lot of oil; it gushed up also at many spots, so that the ground was quite soaked with it; but to one who is not an expert it looked, perhaps, as though they had not succeeded yet in finding the right places where the oil should flow in abundance. Evidently what was needed was a methodical geological survey of the whole ground, so as to bring to light where the faults in the strata give rise to the heaviest oil deposits and then make borings there.

After looking at several springs and borings we drove on towards the coast, and came to one of the large fishing-stations whence fishing is carried on, especially at certain seasons; the most important being the herring fishery. There were great barracks for the fishermen, great sheds with salting-rooms for the herrings, administrative buildings, boats, and so on. Everything had been destroyed during the war, partly by the Russian White troops under Denikin, partly by the English who had fought against the Bolsheviks, and partly by the Turks; they had all been here in turn. The destruction had now been to some extent repaired.

We saw the different kinds of salted herrings, some of them bigger than any herrings I have ever seen. We also tasted them; they are highly salted, but seemed to be fat and good. This was evidently the large Caspian herring, the black-back (*Caspialosa kessleri*), which is found in the deeper waters in the middle part of the Caspian, and in the early spring goes up the rivers, especially the Volga, to spawn. It can be half a metre long and weigh as much as 1½ kilogrammes. There are several smaller kinds of herring found in still greater quantities. The quantity of herrings taken yearly in the Caspian and in the Volga is very great, and they are sold over the whole of Russia. Although these varieties may not come up in quality to our own herring, they make an excellent food for the people.

One of the trawlers just happened to be afloat, a large rowing-boat with an imposing long steering-oar. There were many boats of the same kind ashore, and they looked as if they were strong and well-built craft. But we could not tarry too long; our trip took us farther over the plain, and we were to see some estates that are being worked now by the State. The sun scorched us ruthlessly, the heat was overpowering, and added to this was the constant jolting on the uneven road; it was, indeed, trying. The plain we were here driving over seemed to have a particularly fruitful soil, although it was now half desert owing to the want of water, but in between were marshy, undrained stretches, which evidently were hotbeds of malaria; and there were other tracts of tangled wilderness. The road was in many places almost impassable. For us driving in a carriage it was still practicable; for the car it was worse: often it stuck fast in the boggy ground, and had to be pulled out again; until it stuck quite fast, and those in it had to be driven in a carriage, while the car went home again as soon as it was got out. The buffaloes lay as deep in the water-holes as they could.

We came at last to the great estates, where there were extensive vineyards, besides maize-fields, and, so far as I understood, some cotton-fields. The ground looked to be rich, and in places there was a wealth of vegetation threatening to overgrow all the cultivated land. Especially on the great estate that had belonged to Prince Vorontsov-Dashkov there were valuable vineyards. We came to the buildings, which had suffered greatly during the Revolution. The mansion itself had been wholly destroyed, and the rest of the buildings were also partly in ruins. It was, indeed, the general case that the peasants drove away or killed the owners of estates and destroyed the mansions. We saw the great cellars where the famous wine from this estate was formerly kept; they had partly been destroyed, but were now repaired, and soon the more valuable wine can be laid down in them again.

The estate gave the impression of being a very valuable one with a good soil; and for anyone who knew how to carry it on rationally there were undoubtedly great possibilities there. But now it was partly ruined, and its management evidently suffered from the need of capital to bring it back to its former prosperity. The government, therefore, is very ready to let out the estate under a concession. If the tracts which are now sour were properly drained again, and the irrigation regulated and brought under control, much would already have been done. Malaria was now rife here, and over half the people were said to suffer seriously from it; it hampers their powers of work and their enterprise.

By draining this would be greatly remedied, but besides that a methodical fight would have to be made against the sickness. In this way the people's health and power of work would be raised to a far higher level.

Here, as in many places in these lowlands, we saw small open sleeping-places on high pillars, with a sloping or ridged roof, thatched with rushes or grass. In these they slept at night to get away from the gnats, and also it was cooler and airier there than in the houses, which became heated by the sun in the daytime. In some places we also saw cradles hung up under the same high roofs on pillars, and in them the children lay in the fresh air, safe and well against crawling and flying insects.

Restored by a meal under some shady spreading trees in the courtyard, we drove on. As we came down the great avenue, now overgrown, from the estate, Korkmazov told me of the magnificence and hospitality shown here by the princes in bygone days. A stranger coming there would always find hospitality, and could stay on for days at a time; horses, weapons, and dogs were at his disposal for taking part in sport, and there was good sport of many kinds both in the lowland and up in the mountains : wild boar, pheasants, quail, deer, and others—a glorious country for the sportsman.

The rough road led up and down over the plain towards the coast; we drove fast in our carriage, and were well jolted the whole way. Our destination now was the big new glass-works, built near the railway at a spot where gas comes up out of the ground. It is a large undertaking, meant for an output not only to supply Daghestan, but also a great part of Russia. One of the most costly items in glass-works is the heat for melting the glass, and here this costs nothing, owing to there being the natural gas, which is mainly methane (95 per cent.). It has been streaming up here out of the ground since time beyond memory; near where it now comes up is a platform, which is thought to have been the old altar and holy place of fire-worshippers, where the everlasting fire burned, kept alight by this gas.

Besides the heat for smelting there is also a plentiful supply on the plain near of raw materials needed in glass-making, both pure siliceous and shelly sand. We saw the beds from which it is taken. The works were under the management of Germans from Bohemia, and they seemed to be very capable. For the present only bottle-glass was being made, but the intention was soon to start on window-glass and the finer glass-ware as well. Evidently this industrial undertaking was bound to have a very promising outlook.

The plan was for us to go on farther south from here to the old historic town of Derbent, which for long years was the frontier town between Persia and the warlike nomads (the Scythians, Massagetae, Sakae, etc., and later the Khazar kingdom in the north), and guarded the passage. Besides the difficult and narrow passes through the Caucasus mountains themselves, of which the Darial pass was the most important, the one and only way between the flat land and steppes north of the Caucasus and the eastern lands to the south was over this plain along the Caspian; and at Derbent the steep mountains shut the plain in so that it is at its narrowest. This has been called the Caspian Gate. It was this road that was followed by the wandering peoples from the north, and it was here that the Scythians and others forced their way through in the 7th century B.C. and overcame the Medes (Herodotus, I, 103–106; IV, I).

At Derbent a wall was built 60 to 70 kilometres long, running from the shore over the plain to the foot of the mountains about 600 metres above the Caspian. Like all that is great in this part of the East the wall was attributed to Iskander Beg (that is, Alexander the Great). According to the Arab Yakut-el-Hamavi (about A.D. 1230), the Sassanid king Kobad built a brick wall at Derbent (in Arabian, Bab-el-Abvab = the Gate of Gates) against the Khazars to the north, while his son Anushirvan (A.D. 531–579) built the wall of stone. It still stands in great part. Derbent is the Persian name and means Gate-lock; the Tatar name Temir-kapu means Iron Gate.

Around this town and its wall there has been much fighting through the ages, and many are the legends linked with it. For the Russians in their efforts to push their dominion towards the south-east it was naturally of great moment to have this gateway in their power. As early as 1722 Peter the Great occupied the town during his Persian campaign. It had afterwards to be handed back to

Persia, but thrice the Russians took the town again: in 1775, 1796, and finally in 1806, since when they have kept it. During the late World War and the civil war it suffered much destruction in the fighting against the Turks and the British.

Unfortunately I was suddenly attacked by a serious indisposition, probably due to an infection and the great heat, and I had to go back to Makhach Kalá by train that same evening. It was hard to have to give up Derbent and the interesting programme the Presidents had so hospitably planned out; but their anxiety for my health was truly touching.

I now had to lie quietly and go through a strict milk-cure. But next morning it was announced that a remarkable man had come to greet me. He was the magistrate in an *a-ul* high up in the mountains; he had made a journey to the government at Tiflis, then to Baku, and now had come this way when he heard we were here. I went into the President's reception-room and saw him. He was one of the strongest-built men I have ever seen, over six feet tall, with powerful shoulders and chest and a body in proportion, mighty arms, and hands like scoops, with which he shook mine with great heartiness. He had a large, strong face, wearing a childlike, kindly expression, as is usual with strong men, dark eyes and hair, and somewhat coarse features, reminding one rather of the Nordic type than of the Armenian with its long narrow face. He might have been taken right out of the old tales of giants and berserkers. He was wearing the

Caucasian dress, with high-boots, a belt around his waist, and the usual heavy dagger. So far as I could understand he was a Lesghi. I was told of him that he had carried on his back all the earth for the garden and patches of field that he was now cultivating in the eyry where he dwelt right up among the mountain precipices; it looked as though the back could still carry a good load.

These people, indeed, up in the mountains, have but little ground to till, and therefore in former days, when food grew too scanty, they were wont to make an excursion down below to carry off something from the plain-dwellers. The patches of field that they till generally lie scattered on ledges along the mountain slopes; often there is so little soil that they have to carry it up on their backs, while the patches are small. Korkmazov told us how one day a peasant went up the mountain to work in his field; it was a hot day and when he had come there he threw off his cloak (*burka*). When he looked round for his field he could not find it, it had disappeared; and in the end he had to pick up his cloak to go down again, but there lay the field after all under it.

Although still weak, I had to take a walk next morning (10th of July) down to the shore, and there I could not withstand the temptation to have a swim, which was very refreshing in the heat. Out in the sea one got a strong impression of how the low coastland runs quite flat from the shore up to the foot of the steeply rising mountains. To the north the shore was made up of sand and gravel,

OUR LUNCH ABOVE TARKI

FROM THE LEFT: THE AUTHOR, KORKMAZOV, SAMURSKY, ALI BEG, QUISLING, "THE GENERAL" (STANDING)

THE DANCE AT TARKI

TARKI

but to the south of low cliffs. These flat cliffs were interesting; their top was more or less on the same level all along, and they pierced the layer of loose earth which mainly makes up the plain. It looked as though the cliffs have been planed off through shore erosion at a time when the sea came very much higher, and in this way a so-called "shore-flat" has been formed. The loose layers, too, of the plain were to a great extent laid down under water at a time when the Caspian Sea came higher, and spread its water right up to the mountains. This was at a geological period when the moisture in these parts was far heavier compared with the evaporation than it now is. This was certainly one of the circumstances of the colder climates of the Ice Age. In those times of heavier rainfall the Caspian spread over a vast surface many times as great as the present one, stretching, for instance, over the steppes of south-eastern Russia.

After breakfast we drove in the car south over the plain to the town of Tarki, or Tarku (which is the original and right name). It lies up the steep mountain-side, and was, as we said above, the principal town of the Kumyks, and the seat of their princes or *shamkhals*. When we came to the foot of the mountain we left the cars behind and went up on foot. We went by a remarkable-looking mill, built of stone, with a long flat roof and a heavy overshot wheel. It was clearly a great improvement on the highly primitive mill usually found among the mountain people, which has a horizontal wheel in which the water from a channel spurts

N

against the floats on the side of the wheel and makes this turn horizontally round, while the axle goes straight up to the mill-stone, which is likewise made to turn horizontally. This comes from the time before the device had been found of transforming motion from a horizontal to a vertical axle. There is still an advance to be made from this heavy overshot wheel and to the turbine; but it will come in good time.

The road wound along upwards between leafy trees and gardens which were evidently irrigated with water from the mountain above. Up and up we went, and so we came into the narrow, crooked, and steep streets of the town. The square stone houses with flat roofs stood one above the other up the steep slopes, as usually in the *a-uls* of Daghestan. The houses on the whole seemed comparatively well kept, and the town had the typical look of a thriving *a-ul*. Here and there were some small gardens in among the houses, where there was a big enough ledge and water to irrigate it. There were also trees at many places around the town, but otherwise these mountains, as we have already said, are quite bare and treeless. We saw a bigger house in a comparatively large garden; here the khan or *shamkhal* used once to live.

On a height to the west of the town, and joined to it, rose a fort. The fortress of Burnaya, built by General Velyaminov in 1821, lies on the high mountain above the town. It was, as was said above (p. 129), besieged and nearly taken by Kasi-Mullah after he had captured Tarku in

May 1831. Here also he was buried by the Russians next year, after they had exhibited his body (see p. 133). At a later time Shamyl sent 200 mounted men there by night, who dug up the body and brought it back to Ghimri.

The women here in Tarki go about unveiled; we met many of them in the streets, and could look upon them without offence; indeed, they were so "Christian" that one could even photograph them.

The sun blazed ruthlessly down on us, and it was indeed a hot climb, especially for an invalid. We kept on steadily mounting through the steep streets. In the little market-place we were met by a group of men, among them several of the notables of the town, who welcomed the Presidents and us foreigners. But we soon went on with our climb in the heat. It was pleasant, indeed, to see in a small square in the street a little basin with clear water gushing out of two pipes, and a curious stone erection over it shaped like a beehive; but what this was for I could not find out. Here the pretty young girls met and drew water in their metal pitchers, and men, as pious Mohammedans, performed the prescribed foot-washing.

We had to climb still higher; but then at last we were right up under the perpendicular mountain wall over the town, where a lovely, cold, clear spring came out of the mountain. It was wonderful to lie stretched on one's back by this splashing, cooling water under the shady canopy of leaves, with a wide view over the town at our feet, right away over the plain far below us to the blue sea, and then to dip one's head down and fill one's mouth with the grateful coolness.

It was very touching to see the hospitality of the peasants; they came from the houses below bringing their precious Daghestan rugs, and spread them out on the ground for us to lie on, and they brought pillows and cushions to make us comfortable. Then, when the sad discovery was made that through a mistake in the names our lunch had gone to the town of Talgi (which has mineral springs and baths) down on the plain instead of up here to Tarki, the peasants came up loaded with samovars, bread, butter, eggs, cheese, cherries, and lots besides. It was a lunch that could not have been bettered.

I did not get the impression that this extraordinary hospitality was only due to respect for the two Presidents. It was undoubtedly the natural way of these mountain people, and was meant for us, too, as strangers. And, indeed, we quite forgot any presidential dignity when we were together with our two friends, nor in truth did it weigh them down either. They treated all men as equals, and as such they were also treated themselves.

A half-witted man, "the general" we called him, also made his appearance to welcome us to his land, and to see that everything went on well, and that we were shown the honour that became him and the dignity of his district. He believed himself to be the head of the place. He was equipped with a sabre, and was wearing the Caucasian dress with a light-gray lamb-skin cap, and a long cloak (*cherkeska*) hanging over his breast and shoulders with all kinds of medals and metal badges, even two heavy brass messenger-plates marked "No. 17"; these he said he had got from Stambul.

He had a striking likeness to a half-witted man who in my childhood used to wander from farm to farm in south-eastern Norway. We used to call him "Kaiser Dahl"; he had gone mad when Grue church was burned down and so many perished; he escaped through a window, but could not save his betrothed, who was burned to death inside; he could hear her shrieks. He went about, got up in just the same way as this man, with a sword and cartridge-pouch on a broad strap over his breast, on which hung all kinds of medals and stars, even cotillon favours of gilt paper. What an event it was for us children when he came wandering along and solemnly entered the kitchen, always taking his seat on the same chair; we used to crowd round him to see all the wonderful things he had on him, while he was given food and coffee with lumps of boiled brown sugar in the saucer.

I did not find out how this "general" of ours here had gone mad; but anyhow it is a curious thing that madness in two such different peoples and lands could take forms so like one another. Does it come from a fundamental likeness in the minds of these two peoples, or from a general sameness of human nature? Our "general" said he was not married now, but certainly thought of marrying again; it was not easy, however, to find a likely wife; women were so little to be trusted.

If he heard there was anything we wanted, he at

once gave one of the men standing around an order to fetch it. They would smile, and if anything was really wanted, a messenger was sent for it. He stood there on the look-out down the road, and for him it never seemed to come quickly enough. He bitterly complained that his people did not always at once do his bidding; it was not so easy to carry on the government under such conditions, and much went wrong.

After we had been here a long time I saw two ladies in European clothes with some followers walking up the road that led by the spring. I was surprised to see tourists here, for we had not met any as yet; but now it turned out to be the wives of the two Presidents. They were cordially greeted, and Quisling and I were introduced to Mrs. Korkmazov, an exceedingly lovely and young woman, of whose existence we had not thought, although we lived side by side on the same floor in the President's house. The ladies now stopped, were given carpets to sit on, and became the objects of much attentiveness, especially from "the general".

This day there was to be a wedding with dancing in the town; I wanted to see it and we went down again. As we men were taking leave of the ladies, "the general" with European, or perhaps Eastern, chivalry asked whether he should not stay behind to protect them.

Unfortunately the wedding was all over when we came down; but the dancing on the square before the mosque was still going on. The music was the accordion, and there was always a man and a woman dancing within the ring of onlookers sitting and standing around. This was the Caucasian dance "Lesghinka". The man in Caucasian dress with a sheep-skin cap danced round with quick, rhythmic steps and the arms held out sideways. Then he drew a woman out of the ring; she tripped round staidly with half-bent head before him, coyly shy, while he danced round after her, she always eluding him; this represented the man wooing the woman. Everything was restrained, without any boisterousness. Each of them in his or her way showed a natural grace in all the movements: he manly and strong as he swung round; she shy and womanly, with supple movements. The feet moved with a light quickness like drum-taps in time with the music; they touched backs ever so slightly, while the body was held quite stiff. The dance is something like a Norwegian "springer": the same strong limber movements in the man, and the lissome shyness in the girl; but the rhythm and the position of the feet are not the same, and the man never puts his arm about the woman, or whirls her round as in the "springer"; so near an approach before others would be unthinkable for the Oriental.

But it was growing towards evening, and the sun was setting. While the *muezzin* high up in the minaret was shouting his mournful call to prayer, we walked down through the narrow streets and then the steep road to the mountain-foot, where the cars were waiting. We were whirled along over the plain, and soon we were home again in the

President's house after this fleeting glimpse into the life of the mountains.

Before we went to bed we sat as usual on the balcony in front of the house and drank a glass of tea. It was a still night, and the air felt almost chilly after the fierce heat of the day. On the other side of the street the dark tree-tops lay over the garden, a rustle went once through the leaves like a yearning sigh; high above us was the deep black dome, the stars thick-strewn in all the glory of the south. Inland above the plain rose the wonder-world of the Caucasus with its scattered *a-uls* and the thousands of restless human lives cooped within the mighty mountains. All was wrapped peacefully in care-free dreams under the cloak of night.

It is, as we said, a hard and grinding life in the bare valleys. Indeed, it is hard to imagine one much more grinding, for the very earth that is to be tilled must be carried up and fenced round with stones if it is not to disappear. It might be thought that the people had struggle enough in wresting a bare livelihood from this overpowering world of theirs; but for all that these tribes have always lived at war with one another and with foes from outside. Fighting was their joy. They are like eagles that strike at anyone coming near their eyry, and go far off to win their prey; bold and tough warriors they are beyond compare, but often hard and cruel.

The song of Khochbar of Ghedatl[1] may be

---

[1] English translation by J. F. Baddeley, *op. cit.*, pp. 484–5. Ghedatl was an Avar district near the Avarian Koisu, and south of the khanate.

TARKI AND THE FORT
KORKMAZOV SAMURSKY, ALI BEG, THE AUTHOR

THE WHARF WITH HERRING-BARRELS AT MAKHACH KALA

THE KULUM CANAL IN ASTRAKHAN

brought to mind, whom the Khan Nutsal of Avaria summoned to him. But when the dreaded Khochbar came to Khunsakh as guest, and was received by the khan, six men threw themselves on him and bound him.

"On the long hill-side of Khounzakh they made such a blaze that the very rock grew red-hot beneath it. They brought Khotchbar to the fire; they brought to it his gallant bay steed; they slaughtered it with their swords; they broke in twain his sharp-pointed spear, and threw the pieces into the flames—the hero winked never an eye.

" 'Come now, Khotchbar, sing us something; it is said thou art a master of song. Play us somewhat on the lime-wood cithern; it is said thou playest well.'

" 'Well indeed can I sing; but my mouth is gagged. Well indeed can I play; but my hands are bound.'

"The young men cried out that Khotchbar should be loosed; but the old men said: 'Wolf-deeds we fear from a wolf.'

"The young men had their way; the hero was unbound.

" 'Listen now, men of Khounzakh; I will sing you a song; and thou, O Khan, interrupt me not.'

(He sings to the cithern.)

Who but I clambered in through your window, and carried off the silk trousers of your favourite wife? Who but I took the silver bracelets from the white arms of your complacent sisters? Who but I cut the throat of your tame Tour? [1]

---

[1] Mountain goat, *capra caucasica*.

There, above, are the sheep-folds; who drove the sheep away? Why are they empty? There, below, is the stable; Who drove the horses off? Where are they now? Lo, on the house-tops, the widows! Who killed their husbands and made them such? Orphans I see around me. Who slew their sires and orphaned them? None can count the number of those who have died by my hands in the fields, in the forest. I have slaughtered no less than three-score men of your tribe. These are deeds, O Noutsal, worthy of fame; but to take a man by fraud and kill him—what shall we say of that?

"While Khotchbar played and sang, the two little sons of the Khan came round and sat at his feet. Snatching them up suddenly, one in each hand, the hero leapt into the flames.

Why shriek, ye Noutsal cubs? Do not *I* burn with you?
Why squeal, ye piglings? Did not *I* too love the light?
Alas! for my gallant bay, that trampled so oft the heels
of the flying Avars. Alas! for my pointed lance, that
pierced full oft the breasts of the Noutsal's henchmen.
Weep not, mother mine—not vainly your darling dies.
Let not my sisters greet—I perish gloriously.

"There was scraping of viols and beating of drums from morn till noon; Khotchbar of Ghedatl was taken.

"There was weeping and wailing when noon was past; the Avar princes had perished in the flames."

What impassive witnesses, indeed, have not these mountains been of adventures, fighting, toil, robbery, self-sacrifice, love, sorrow, and always and again toil! All of us are striving; we fight, live, suffer—and a hundred years hence? The mountains are there, they are the same; but what of the men and women, and their plans and dreams?

Our friends, the two Presidents, had conceived the curious idea that I might be of some use in advising as to the working of Daghestan's economic possibilities, of which I had now seen a great deal. My objection that this lay somewhat outside my experience was of no avail. Clearly, if the potentialities so far lying unworked could be turned into money, best of all through concessions, it would be a great help to this very poor people, whose whole budget was about 10,000,000 roubles.

Next day (11th of July) there was, therefore, a great meeting of the whole of the Daghestan commissariat to discuss these questions. During our excursions I had already more than once said that I quite understood there might be valuable mineral wealth such as oil, natural sulphur in great quantities, and perhaps metals also in the mountains; but still it seemed to me that the land must always find its incomparably greatest wealth in the broad rich plain on which we now were, and which runs 216 kilometres northwards by the delta of the Terek to the frontier at the Kuma, covering over 25,000 square kilometres. It is true that there were many salt steppes there in the north; but a great part of this plain could surely be brought under cultivation, so far as I could see. Once the hundreds of thousands of *dessyatins* of fertile land lying here more or less fallow had been drained and irrigated, and brought under the plough, they could beyond

all doubt be transformed into the most splendid
fields and gardens, with cotton, fruit, silk-groves,
tobacco, vegetables, vineyards—not to speak of
corn. This, too, did not look to be any really
impossible task. In the north they had the river
Terek, which, so far as I understood, was particularly
fitted for irrigation; while here, farther south, there
were plenty of streams coming down from the
mountains, and water could be led from them over
the plain. For ploughing this flat land motor-
ploughs could be used with great advantage here,
where they had petroleum.

One great difficulty, of course, was the malaria.
It must be fought methodically, and on this the commissariat was quite definite. But the opening up of
the land to cultivation, and especially the draining
of the stretches of swamp, would in themselves be a
very great help in this direction; and besides, other
effective methods could be brought into play—such as
the spraying of marshes and all standing water with
naphtha, which here, where naphtha lies to hand,
would not cost much more than the labour needed.

As to all this the commissariat was fully agreed;
and although they had been of the opinion that
their main resources lay in the richness of the
various minerals, they had now gone over to the
view that efforts should mainly be directed to
bringing this flat land under cultivation. But how
was this to be done? A work such as this on a great
scale, with draining, irrigation, and so forth, must
have capital, and Daghestan was a poor land that
could not make great economic efforts.

Two courses seemed open: either to try to raise a loan for Daghestan to be used for bringing the land under cultivation, a loan which could evidently be easily paid back from the profits on this land; or else to grant foreigners concessions of land for cultivation. Many of the commissars held that a loan for Daghestan would entail difficulties, since the republic was not financially independent but part of the Socialist-Soviet Republic in Moscow. It was held, therefore, that the simplest and easiest thing would be to arrange concessions, if possible. They had formerly had a German colony in the north of this plain; and the colonists had got on well, and were liked by all. During the war, unfortunately, they had been driven out, but the commissariat would have very much liked to have such settlers again, and would have been grateful for anything that might be done in this direction. They wished, too, to have help in the fight against malaria, and in buying tractors. If only they could find the means of bringing these plains under cultivation, there would be no need to bring in settlers; there were enough people up in the mountains, where they were so badly off for patches of soil.

In truth, there were plenty of openings here, and good grounds for anyone giving valuable help, so long as he had the power and the will. We have only to think how in Western Europe there is unemployment everywhere and a difficulty in earning enough to keep life together; while here is the land only waiting to be worked to yield a goodly harvest. We have only to think that if the right men could once be found to start work, so much room could be made here for new homes, and for thousands and thousands of people that are now more or less workless, and could become useful producers. There is more than enough room here on this little earth, if only it were shared out and made use of with some intelligence.

After the meeting there was a great breakfast with the whole of the commissariat; all these Mohammedans drank wine, and there were many eloquent speeches on the fruits of our co-operation and on the future of Daghestan.

IX

OVER THE CASPIAN TO ASTRAKHAN

OVER THE CASPIAN TO ASTRAKHAN

Quisling and I would gladly have made a long stay in this interesting country among its sympathetic people if only there had been time; and it was with regret that in the afternoon we drove to the steamer that was to take us over the Caspian to the Volga. Our kind friends the two Presidents, Samursky and Korkmazov, and others of the commissariat went on board with us. We now said good-bye to our hosts, who had shown us what was meant by the renowned hospitality of their land. The utmost thought was given to our comfort on the overladen boat, and an array of gifts was sent us on board worthy of an Eastern prince.

The boat came from Baku and was full of passengers bound north for Astrakhan; many, too, came aboard at Makhach Kalá, and the landing-stage was packed tight with people and crowded with row after row of herring-barrels piled on one another. Then at last we were off, our hosts accompanying us some way out in a small tug to wave a last good-bye. Makhach Kalá on its plain, with the blue wall of the Caucasus behind, sank slowly below the blue surface of the sea in the evening.

On this steamer we had come again into a new world. The many passengers seemed to be mostly Russians; but what struck us like something new after we had been travelling in the Caucasian world was the comparatively great number of women among them, and the free way they associated with the men, like comrades on an equal footing. All ages were here, and several young loving couples, who may well have been on their honeymoon.

The water we steamed through is quite shallow, mostly under ten metres deep, like the whole, northern part of the Caspian. Next morning (12th of July) we came to the still shallower part off the Volga delta, where we shifted over into a paddle-boat, for the channel through the delta has only about 2 metres depth. The sea was here quite covered by the golden-brown muddy water of the river, which spreads over the salt water. As we steamed up we passed many small lightships, and saw many great barges, like islands with a house on them. Often there was a line of them, one behind the other, drawn by a tug; on some of the barges a square yard-sail was set to help the tug as they went north. We also passed some two-masted sailers; with a fair wind they were sailing the same course as ours, some laden with dried *vobla*, which lay in great heaps on the deck. It reminded me of the Norland coasters years ago which sailed to Bergen with dried fish piled up high among the bulwarks. *Vobla* or roach is the fish which is most caught here, and the whole peasantry lives on it. It is a variety (*Rutilus rutilus caspicus*) of our common freshwater roach (*Leuciscus rutilus*, L.), from which it is distinguished by being a salt-water and migratory fish. It is found throughout the

Caspian Sea, especially in its northern part.[1]
In its reproductive period it grows to be 12 to 36
centimetres long, and weighs 70 to 500 grammes,
according to its age. Early in spring, in April and
May, and as soon as the ice breaks up, it comes up
into the Volga delta in vast quantities to spawn.
It is the most important product of the fisheries,
and is mostly lightly salted, and then dried on
stages on huge drying-grounds. The yearly catch
is 600 to 1,000 million fish, weighing 82,000 to
150,000 tons. Vobla is cheap and easy to freight
when dried, and together with the herring it makes
the most important food of the people in Russia.

The low flat islands and shoals in the del a were
a fresh green on both sides from the reeds. Clumps
of trees, and churches with small hamlets around
them, could be seen far away over the lowland,
which did not rise much above the surface of the
water. The land is cut in every direction by
branches of the river, and is swampy and full of
malaria. Farther north the land stood a little
higher above the river, especially on the west side,
though never many metres. The river seemed still
to be running fairly high, but becomes lower later
on in the summer. At Astrakhan it is generally
highest about the middle of June; and then it sinks
steadily till the low-water period in September.
The villages gradually grew in size, and now lay
in some cases right on the slightly higher west bank

[1] The information given here and below about the fishes is taken
from Professor Arvid Behning's excellent book, *Das Leben der Wolga*,
in A. Thienemann, *Die Binnengewässer*, vol. v; Stuttgart, 1928.

of the arm of the river by which we were coming up, which was also the most westerly one in the delta. As usual great churches stood high above the low houses of the villages, the houses often spreading far around.

Over the green reedy shores flew birds that looked just like big black duck, but which are not much eaten, it was said; there are said to be, however, plenty of other kinds of duck, and splendid duck- and goose-shooting. When the water is at its average height you can wade for kilometres over the reedy flats of the delta, especially to the east of where we were; the water does not reach more than half-way up the shank, and there are great quantities of wild duck and geese in these reeds.

The channel up was shallow and difficult all the time, with sand-banks everywhere; but the course was well buoyed. There was a lively traffic on the river, and it grew as we came nearer to Astrakhan; one had the impression of approaching one of the great trading centres. There were many fishing boats everywhere, and strings of heavy lighters in tow; often three were tied up together at the bows side by side in a bunch, as it were, so that their sterns tailed out sideways as they were towed up. One was more and more struck by the fact that the land on the west side of the channel grew higher, while on the east it was low and swampy.

ASTRAKHAN

At half-past eight in the evening we reached Astrakhan, half an hour too late to catch the passenger-boat up the Volga. Comrade Tarkhov, chief of the executive committee in the province of Astrakhan, came on board to welcome us; with him came also the head of all the shipping lines here. They told us we must wait and go by the express boat next evening, for the one that went at ten o'clock that same evening was a mixed goods and passenger boat and much slower. But we could shift over at once to the express boat, as it was lying near. It was a splendid roomy paddle-boat, and we were given the coolest and largest cabin I think I have ever seen on any ship, as high as an hotel ashore. Everything looked promising.

With Comrade Tarkhov and his friend we then went to a summer theatre in a large garden, where an operetta was being given. The house was full, and it was interesting to watch the many pro-menaders in the garden in the long intervals. They mostly gave the impression of belonging to a prosperous working class, but with a sprinkling of others; the ladies were quite well dressed.

The next morning (13th of July) a car was put at our disposal, and we drove round the town. It has over 175,000 inhabitants, and from olden times has been an important trading town for this part of the world. It is extraordinarily well placed here at the mouth of the Volga as a transit harbour for all the trade and traffic to and from the immense area belonging to the mighty river and waterway, and to and from the Caspian, whose hinterland is also very great, especially when we bear in mind the Trans-Caspian Railway to the rich lands in the

East. The town, moreover, is the centre for the great fisheries in the Volga delta and the northern-most part of the Caspian.

As early as the first centuries of our era the Khazars had founded an important trading town, Itil, on the right bank of the Volga about 10 kilometres above Astrakhan; and it came to be the market and meeting-place for traders from Byzantium, Baghdad, Armenia, and Persia, as also from the Volga and the Don, and the lands to north and west. It was hither, too, that the Khazar capital was shifted from Semender (later known as Tarku), near the Caucasus, at the end of the 7th century, after the Arab invasion of Caucasia. Here were brought wax, skins, leather, and honey from up the Volga. When the Jews were turned out of Constantinople they made their way to Itil and developed the trade for the Khazars, and likewise spread their faith in rivalry with the Mohammedans and Christians. The dynasty embraced the Jewish faith about A.D. 740.

The Khazars were the leading middle-men between East and West; but then, after many ups and downs, their power became lessened by the Varangian-Russian kingdom at Kiev; and when Ibn Fadhlân visited Khazaria about A.D. 922, Itil was, indeed, still a great town with baths, market-places, and thirty mosques, but there was no great production or activity at home; the kingdom depended on the somewhat uncertain transit tolls. Then in 965-9 Itil, Semender, and other towns were taken by Prince Svyatoslav of

Kiev. Itil (or Balanyar, as it was called after the destruction by the Russians in 969) was then utterly destroyed by Tamerlane at the end of the 14th century; and later Astrakhan was founded where it now stands, and became the capital of a Tatar khanate until it was taken by the Russians under Ivan the Terrible in 1557, since when it has been Russian always. In 1660 it withstood the siege by the Tatars, but in 1670 it was taken by Stenka Razin. Peter the Great made the town the base for his campaign against Persia, built ship-yards there, and contributed to its growth. It is now used by several thousand ships a year, and its outward and inward trade is important.

The most important source of food supplies for the town and the whole district is beyond comparison the rich fisheries, and more than half the population lives by them. The canal through the town, and a tributary (the Kulum) of the river, offered a picturesque sight with the crowds of boats along the banks. We visited the market-place, where there was a busy traffic; all kinds of wares were on sale on tables in small booths, or on trays. Every kind of natural type was there: Russians, Tatars, Persians, Kirghizes. The many women, both buyers and sellers, made an ever-present contrast to Tiflis.

On the highest spot in the town we saw the Kremlin, with the white wall around it, loopholed and with several towers. Within the wall is also the cathedral with five green domes. In the street before the entrance tower to the Kremlin on the east side there was formerly the great bazaar; it is now in ruins as a result of the revolutionary wars. The English at that time bombarded the town from five aeroplanes, and are said to have done great damage. We also saw various ruined houses in the town, but I do not think it is so sure that all this damage should be put down only to the English.

After having also visited the Tatar bazaars, where they were sitting at work, we drove to the government building, where, as always in these great administrative buildings of the Soviet Republic, there sat a crowd of functionaries in every room, and there was a never-ending running to and fro. I have always been puzzled how these people can manage to work amid all this noise; but perhaps the truth is that the Russians are wont to make use of even more persons for the administration than we do, and so considerably less work falls on each one of them. We were received by our friend from yesterday, Tarkhov, who took us over to the State bank. Here we were initiated into the work of the bank, which has as its main object to help the fisheries; this was done by granting every kind of fishery undertaking loans on the cheapest possible terms. We were given the clear impression that the authorities looked on it as of the utmost importance for the welfare and progress of the community to foster and support private enterprise, and especially so among the fishermen.

After lunch had also been served up on the green table, with caviare, which can hardly be fresher than it is here in its own home, we went down to

216

the wharves along the Volga and saw the fish-vats on the lighters. In them were quantities of live fish of different kinds; these were taken up wriggling and struggling, in great nets, and when the fish wanted had been picked out, the rest were put in again. There were several sturgeon of the two kinds *ossetrina* and *sevryuga* of various sizes; but there were none of the really big ones. The biggest of all sturgeon is the *beluga* or isinglass-sturgeon (*Acipenser huso*, L.), which can be over five metres long and weigh over a ton. In former times it was caught even up to nearly two tons.[1] It yields much very excellent caviare, and the meat is highly esteemed, both fresh and smoked. The air-bladder yields the valuable isinglass and glue. This sturgeon lives in the Caspian and in the Black Sea, and goes up the big rivers, especially the Volga, to spawn in the following spring. As it is of very slow growth, and does not spawn oftener than every second or third year, it does not increase so fast as it is fished, although the female fish lays up to two and a half million eggs; its numbers, therefore, have been gradually lessening of late years. In the Volga it is caught with coarse-meshed nets, but it is mainly caught in the northern part of the Caspian. Before the war about 76,000 were caught yearly, that is, 44,000 tons; and this yielded 1,200 tons of caviare.

The ossetrina (*Acipenser güldenstädti*) is a good deal smaller than the isinglass-sturgeon; it runs up to 2 metres in length, seldom more, and weighs up to 100 kilogrammes; usually it is about 1½ metres and

[1] As to this and the following kinds, cp. A. Behning, *op. cit.*, pp. 74 ff.

weighs 15 to 25 kilogrammes. It is found throughout the Caspian, and goes up the rivers, especially the Volga, to spawn in the following May; each female fish yields 80,000 to 800,000 eggs. Today about 200,000 young fish are also artificially hatched out yearly. Of this kind of sturgeon about 300,000 to 400,000 are caught yearly, or up to 5,000 tons.

An ossetrina was brought up for us from one of the vats and opened. It was full of roe in two long thick strands on each side of the belly; there must have been quite a couple of kilogrammes of caviare in this one fish. As is well known, caviare is prepared by stirring about in the roe with a small stick or a spoon, until all the pieces of skin have been taken out and each grain is left free. It is then ready to be eaten fresh and gets the highest prices, especially that of the beluga, but also that of the ossetrina and of the sevryuga. The ossetrina caviare is generally lightly salted and pressed, so as to be more easily sent away, and then it will keep quite a long time. It is what is known as *payusnaya ikra*.

The sevryuga or star-sturgeon (*Acipenser stellatus*, Pall.) is usually much smaller than the ossetrina, seldom reaching 2 metres length and 50 kilogrammes weight. It is mostly 1 to 1½ metres, weighing up to 12 kilogrammes. The great bulk of this sturgeon swims up the Kura and the Ural river to spawn, but many, too, swim up the Volga. This sturgeon spawns in May and June, a female fish laying from 35,000 to 360,000 eggs. Of late years from four to five million artificially hatched fry are put yearly into the Volga. The yearly catch in the Volga and in the Caspian near the delta is about 600,000 fish, weighing 2,500 to 3,300 tons. It is this kind that yields the best salted caviare (*payusnaya*).

There is another sturgeon to be mentioned: the *sterlet* (*Acipenser ruthenus*), which is found all along the Volga from the delta as far as its upper waters; it is, however, altogether a freshwater fish. It is smaller than the other kinds of sturgeon, sometimes reaching a length of one metre and a weight of 16 kilogrammes; but usually the fish caught are about 35 to 55 centimetres. It is highly thought of as the finest fish in the Volga, and makes the celebrated *ukha* (fish-soup); it is also served whole, boiled, baked, cold, smoked, and in other ways. About 32 millions are caught every year along the whole river. The caviare is smaller than in the other kinds of sturgeon, and is not sent away, but eaten on the spot quite fresh.

After this Comrade Shvedov, vice-president of the executive committee, took us over the Volga in a small steamboat; there was a lively traffic of ships and boats, fishing-boats, steamers, and lighters with tugs. We were taken to a place on the right bank of the river where there were great long fishing-sheds which were regular ice-houses. They have double walls, and the space between is filled right up to the roof with ice in winter. This ice melts slowly in the summer, and keeps these great rooms so cold that many of us were frozen when we came in from the heat outside, and we did not stay long.

In great chambers underground the herrings which had come in from last spring's fishing were kept laid in salt. Here were stored 100,000 poods (1,640 tons) of fish; but there was room for 150,000 poods. These herrings were now ready to be put in casks and sent all over Russia. From each storage-shed a long jetty or slip sloped down into the water for bringing ashore the fresh fish from the boats and for bringing out the salted fish for loading.

We went back over the Volga again, and so into one of its arms a little north of the town, and going east. Here we passed great storage-yards for timber, and along the bank lay ever so many timber-rafts in a row that had come down the Volga. Timber, it is needless to say, is valuable in this treeless land. After passing under the railway bridge we came to two great ice and refrigerating factories. Instead of natural ice, of which there is more than enough here in winter, being used for preserving, especially for preserving herrings on the other side of the river, artificial ice and cold is made here by machinery for preserving the valuable kinds of fresh fish; this rich land can also easily get its supply of oil for power. One Russian factory is worked by Diesel motors, and in it there are frozen and preserved 500,000 poods (8,200 tons) of fresh fish of various kinds, such as sturgeon (beluga, ossetrina, sevryuga, sterlet), various kinds of freshwater fish, such as pike-perch or *sudak* (*Lucioperca lucioperca*), bream, and so forth. Besides this there is a former English refrigerating factory here, worked by steam with oil fuel, where 250,000 poods (4,100 tons) of fresh fish are frozen and stored. This fish is constantly being sent out all over Russia in cold-storage wagons on the railways.

When we were to go down to see the great freezing-rooms we were advised to put on furs, which were there for this purpose; but this seemed quite absurd; in this oppressive heat a short cooling would be refreshing. I soon repented, and gave up the visit to the coldest rooms. The brave Quisling went on and stood it; it was indeed cold, he said.

Fresh fish was brought daily to these refrigerating factories from the fishing that goes on all the time in the Volga and its delta; on the wharves in front of them there was much movement, with many boats unloading their catch: pike-perch (sudak), ossetrina, sevryuga, roach, herring, etc.

We had now seen the most important of the activities of Astrakhan, and could come back south again in our little steamboat along the wharves to the shady deck of our passenger-boat, where a cool drink was refreshing beyond belief in this heat.

X

THE VOLGA

THE VOLGA

The Fisheries

We had received a strong impression of the great importance of the fisheries for the people here. Taken all together, the huge quantities of fish of different kinds that are caught during the year (but mostly in the spring and early summer) in the Volga delta and the shallows outside it, only a few metres deep, make up something which is unparalleled.

Along with the vobla fishery mentioned above, the herring fishery here at the mouth of the Volga is the greatest and most important. The Caspian species of herrings or "May fish" belong to a specific genus, *Caspialosa*, standing near the genus *Alosa*, to which belongs the largest species of herring, the prototype of the herring (*Alosa vulgaris*, Cuv.), running up to 60 centimetres. It is found along the shores of Europe, and goes up the rivers to spawn; most of the Caspian species of herring do the same, or anyhow they go up into the fresh water in or off the Volga delta.

The most important species for the fishery is the Volga herring (*Caspialosa volgensis*).[1] This migrates in a body up into the Volga delta at the beginning of May to spawn in May and June; the passage lasts five to seven days, during which the fishing is mainly carried on, often with huge catches. It comes in great numbers right up to Stalingrad (Tsaritsin),

[1] As to this and the following species, cp. A. Behning, *op. cit.*, pp. 78 ff.

and sometimes even much farther. Of these herrings it is only a minority that falls victim to the poor condition resulting from the migration and spawning. The others go back to the sea, and may once more go up the river to spawn, but they do not seem to spawn more than twice. This herring matures after three years, and does not live much over six. About 450 millions are caught yearly, weighing 150,000 tons.

The largest species of Caspian herring, the "black-back" (*Caspialosa kessleri*), up to half a metre long and weighing up to 1½ kilogrammes, has already been spoken of (p. 105). It goes up the Volga in early spring, and reaches Samara at the beginning or towards the middle of June. It comes to above the Kama and the Oka, and may go another 1,290 kilometres up the Kama. The spawning females are five to six years old, and spawn only once. After the spawning they all, both males and females, perish from exhaustion after the long journey; and in the years when there have been great quantities of them, it is said to be a wonderful sight, when the high water falls, to see the dead herrings hanging in huge numbers on the osiers and the willow-bushes, now left dry. The fishing is mainly in the arms of the delta, through which the fish swims up. In 1911–15, 20 millions was the yearly catch, but now it is very much less, for the quantity that goes up is no longer so great. That number yielded some 15,000 tons of salted herring; only a small part, mostly taken from the largest fish, is smoked.

Of importance also is the Caspian herring (*Caspialosa caspia*). Of this fish only a part goes up the Volga delta to spawn; the main body spawns about the end of May or in June in the fresh water off the delta, or in the many *limans* or cut-offs on its west side. The yearly catch of this herring is about 130 millions, or 17,500 tons. The other varieties of herrings in the Caspian are of less importance for the fisheries. There is also a species like the brisling (*Harengula delicatula*) that spawns in or off the Volga delta at the end of April and the beginning of May. It has not been fished, but perhaps will be used for preserving at some time in the future.

An interesting fish, which is also caught in the Volga, is the Caspian lamprey (*Caspiomyzon wagneri*). This lowly eel-like fish with a sucker-mouth lives mostly on the bottom and in the mud, and goes up the Volga from the sea from September to December; after swimming 2,000–2,400 kilometres up the river it spawns in April to May. It is caught in a kind of eel-basket, and was formerly used for cattle-feed or melting down the fat; it is now usually baked or pickled. The yearly catch is about 20–30 millions, weighing 1,140–2,130 tons.

Of no little importance are the true fresh-water fishes, that is, above all, carp, sheat-fish (or wels), pike, and perch, which are found throughout the Volga and its tributaries in many varieties, and are fished over a great distance. As opposed to the sturgeons, which are called "red" or "splendid" fish, they are called "white" fish because of their white meat. A peculiar biological group of these species of fishes is found in the Volga delta, and sometimes also in the brackish water in the Caspian just off the delta. In the delta they are called "pit-fish", because in the winter they lie low in "pits" or deeps of 4–5 metres in the arms of the delta near its mouth. These fishes, which have had plenty of food in the summer, swarm together in huge numbers in these "pits", the big fish such as the sheat-fish (*Silurus glanis*) deepest and in the middle, the roach at the side, and the carp and bream between them. As, owing to the water's low winter temperature (nearly 0° C.), metabolism is slow, they lie in a kind of torpid state. Luckily these places are strictly preserved in winter, other-wise the fishermen, who know the places exactly, would easily destroy every single fish. A proof of this was seen during the Revolution in 1917, when all this area was so fished out that it was five to six years before the stock of fish could renew itself in some degree, and in the first years after this the fish had nearly disappeared. In the early spring the fish wake, and come up from the pits into the nearest parts of the delta, spawning among the reeds in the flooded land of the lower delta. After now living on the rich food here, later on with the growing volume of fresh water they move up to 100 kilometres out into the sea, and towards autumn they again make for the delta. The yearly catch of these fish in the Volga delta is about as follows: carp 13,000 tons, bream 19,000, sheat-fish 4,000, pike-perch (sudak, *Lucioperca lucioperca*) 20,000, blick (*Blicca björkna*) 8,500, and rudd (*Aspius aspius*) 1,200 tons; that is, altogether 65,700 tons.

Mention must also be made of the white salmon

(*Stenodus leucichthys*) fishery; this is a very good fish, and differs little from the highly esteemed white salmon or *nelma* (*Stenodus leucichthys nelma*) of the north Russian and Siberian rivers falling into the Arctic Sea. It is found mostly in the north of the Caspian; to some extent it goes up the Volga in late autumn and winter, but the main body begins to migrate later in the winter or at the very first melting of the ice. It comes far up the Kama in great numbers, as far as Vishera and Ufa, to spawn there at the end of September and in October. after a migration of 2,700-2,800 kilometres. After spawning, most of the fish go back to the sea; but now they are extremely thin, for they eat very little throughout their journey in the river. Many, especially the female fish, do indeed perish from exhaustion. The white salmon can reach a length of 110 centimetres and a weight of 16 kilogrammes. It reaches maturity when five to six years old, and is then 70-90 centimetres long, and now starts on its migration up the rivers. A female fish lays about 170,000 eggs. Of late years 2-10 millions of fry are artificially hatched out. The white salmon fishery is of no small value; this is so especially because of its fat, well-tasting, and boneless meat, and also because the fishery is mainly carried on in the winter, when the fish keeps well. Before the war the yearly catch on the lower Volga was 35,000-50,000 fish, that is, 280-410 tons. For comparison we may state that here in Norway the salmon and salmon-trout fishery along the whole of our long coast and in the rivers yields 570-1,150 tons a year.

There is still another variety of salmon, the Caspi-Black Sea salmon (*Salmo trutta labrax*), in the Caspian, near akin to our salmon-trout; it is found mostly in the more southerly parts of the sea, and goes up the rivers along the west coast between Terek and Sefid-Rud in Persia. Occasionally it comes up the Volga along with the white salmon; it is generally 80–100 centimetres long, weighing about 20 kilogrammes.

We may mention here also that in the north of the Caspian, north of the Manghishlak peninsula, the Caspian seal is hunted, 40,000 being taken yearly.

In accordance with what has been said above we have the following table of the quantities of fish taken yearly in the Volga delta and the neighbouring waters of the Caspian, and on the lower Volga:

	Tons
Volga herring and other kinds of herring, in all	183,000
Vobla	82,000–150,000
Freshwater fish ("white fish")	65,700
Isinglass-sturgeon (beluga)	44,000
Russian sturgeon (ossetrina)	5,000
Star sturgeon (sevryuga)	2,500–3,300
Lampret	1,140–2,130
White salmon	280–410
Total	384,120–454,040

For comparison it may be stated that in Norway all the rich fisheries of every kind of fish along the whole of our long coast-line yield altogether 438,000–799,000 tons a year; and on an average for seventeen years (1910–27) they yielded about 599,000 tons yearly. The yearly yield of our herring fisheries alone is 300,000–400,000 tons; the great

Scottish herring fisheries in 1924, a good year, yielded 470,000 tons. Compared with these figures, the amount of fish caught near the mouth of the Volga alone is seen quite to hold its own; all this fish finds its food and lives and grows in the northernmost, shallow part of the Caspian, especially near to and in the Volga delta; while it is only a small part of the migrating swarms that finds its food in the Volga itself. There is, indeed, a highly remarkable production of various kinds of fish in a relatively small area, and this suggests that there must be a lavish and unparalleled supply of plankton and fish-food in this part of the sea. This, perhaps, may be best explained by assuming that the Volga's golden-brown flood, that is ever pouring out into this sea, holds in it rich supplies above the ordinary of feeding-matter, especially, perhaps, nitrogen compounds (nitrates, nitrites, etc.) favouring the growth of plant-plankton, and thereby of animal-plankton and fish-food as well. The Volga in all its length of 3,694 kilometres flows through a vast expanse of flat and fertile land, overlaid to a great extent by the "black earth" so extraordinarily rich in humus; and the river receives tributaries from a huge area covering 1,459,000 square kilometres. Owing to the great rise in this mighty stream (up to 15 metres or more) every spring and early summer, it overflows the low fertile land for a great distance, and its waters carry with them great quantities of nitrogenous feeding-products from the highly cultivated land-surfaces. But in the flowing waters there is not the time nor the conditions for these products to help form a rich plankton; and the greater part of them are thus carried out unused into the Caspian. In the Caspian there are no strong currents of any width, nor any tides to distribute this river water over a large area, as happens in the case of the usual open sea-coast; thus it collects in the northern and shallow part of this sea, especially near the Volga delta.

The volume of water carried by the Volga in its lower reaches may vary, according to calculations, between 1,200 and about 60,000 cubic metres (tons) a second. This means that in the summer when the water is high it carries something like 200 million cubic metres of water an hour, or 5,000 million cubic metres in twenty-four hours, out into the Caspian. In other words, every twenty-four hours it could cover an area of 2,500 square kilometres with water to the depth of 2 metres. This water is always bringing fresh supplies of valuable feeding-matter, and together with the favourable warmth (up to 26°–28° C. in the summer) yields the conditions needed for the growth of an extraordinarily rich plankton-life, which in turn brings about the growth and development of the fish. This is probably the explanation of why it would be hard to find another such place where anything like so great quantities of fish, and of various kinds, are caught in so limited an area.

Up the Volga

Before we left Astrakhan in the evening Mr. Strelnikov, the owner of the barge with vats which we had been aboard, had without our knowing it brought us to the steamer two large cases of fine caviare from the ossetrina which we had seen opened, and had got the captain to put them in the ship's cold chamber. Our Soviet hosts had also sent aboard a large supply of pressed caviare; I brought some of it home with me to Norway, which kept very well in spite of the summer heat.

At eight o'clock in the evening (13th of July) we left for the north up the Volga in our roomy and comfortable boat, which had a fine large promenade-deck. Comrade Shvedov and our other hosts followed a little of the way in a tug.

Thus we started on a remarkable journey up this river, the largest in Europe, and the mighty artery of the Russian plain, which with its tributaries waters most of the Russian Soviet Republic west of the Urals—a plain of 1,459,000 square kilometres, or more than Germany, France, and Great Britain taken together. This area, with over 50 million inhabitants, was before the World War Europe's granary, and it was from here and the Ukraine that, among others, our own land Norway took most of its imported corn. The amount of corn grown there has not yet been brought back again to a level allowing of much to be exported.

The Volga is the source of well-being for the people in the whole of south-east Russia; along it and its tributaries you can go by boat right up to the Ural mountains in the east, through canals to the Polar Sea in the north and to the Baltic in the north-west, and, when the Don canal is finished, to the Black Sea and the Mediterranean in the south-west. As it is now, there is steamship connection almost all the way from the Baltic to the Caspian. Of the 130 tributaries of the Volga, there are twelve navigable, and the whole distance of its navigable waters is 29,770 kilometres.

Starting from its source in the Valdai heights in the province of Tver in the north-west, the Volga, over a length of 3,694 kilometres, falls altogether 262 metres to the Caspian Sea; but mostly it runs through a flat land, so that the average speed of its current is small, usually about 0·80–1·2 metres a second, or 2·9–4·3 kilometres an hour. When the water is high, the speed may rise to over twice as much, but when the water is low in autumn it becomes much less than this average. It has been found that the melting water in the spring takes fifty days to flow from Rybinsk to Astrakhan, a distance of 2,747 kilometres. This gives a speed of about 2·3 kilometres an hour, or 0·64 metre a second. In its lower part, south of Samara and Saratov, the breadth of the river reaches 2 kilometres or more; with its delta it comes out into the Caspian 170 kilometres broad.

Up and down this mighty waterway there is an unceasing movement of innumerable boats, ships, rafts, lighters, and steamers, with thousands of people, and with precious cargoes of the crops and products of the rich land. Along the banks lie many wealthy and large towns, with the bustle and noise of human life. In various stretches of its long valley and plain great and mighty kingdoms have in course of time been founded, once more to fall to ruin—such as the Bulgars in Bulgary, the Khazars in the south, the Mongols, the Tatars, and others, until the Russians established their power from the north and the west. But the Volga in its broad winding bed bears its mighty yellow-brown flood through the flat broad plain as it has done through thousands of years, and did long before man showed himself. The only result to be seen from man's presence is that the forests, which held back the moisture, have been more and more cut down, and thus the river-floods, when the snow melts in spring, have been swollen, but they have also become short-lasting.

The lively traffic on the Volga goes mostly up the river towards the Baltic; and the canal joining it up with the Neva has made Leningrad the chief port for the Volga. To Leningrad fifteen times as much goods is shipped as to Astrakhan, mostly fish, metals, manufactured goods, hides, corn, flour, flax, petroleum, oils, salt, and timber. The goods that are shipped down the river are mostly manufactured ones, and also timber for the treeless provinces of Samara, Saratov, and Astrakhan. Many barges, too, are broken up for their timber after making the journey once down the river with a load.

The river is always changing its course, and has to be dredged every year. Ships often run on to the sand-banks; near the most dangerous ones there are generally steamers stationed to help them off again.

In former days there were tens of thousands of haulers (*burlaki*), who used to drag the boats and barges along the banks up the river, and it is from them that the well-known Volga songs come; but now in the day of the tug-boat these haulers are found only along some of the tributaries. For towing along the canals horses are used.

All this shipping activity and busy water-traffic on the Volga lasts through the summer and autumn. But then the temperature sinks, a temperature which in July reaches 25°–26° C. in the water south of Saratov, and in the delta and about Astrakhan up to 28·5° C. It gradually draws near to 0° C., and in November ice begins to form; the river little by little loses all its life, and all shipping movements come to an end. But as soon as the ice is thick enough, it makes for three or four months a splendid highway for a lively sledge-traffic up and down the river, or across it. The railways, too, make use of it; rails are laid from bank to bank at places where are no bridges, and so the goods-wagons are taken over without the costly use of ice-breakers. The ice reaches an average thickness of 70–90 centimetres, but may even be 1·5 metres on the lower Volga. In the spring the ice breaks up again about the 10th–20th of April on the lower Volga, and about the 14th of March at Astrakhan, and the drift-ice comes with its huge floating masses, which pile themselves up high along the banks; woe then to the boat that is not lying well sheltered! This lasts for a week or two, and then the Volga is open again for traffic.

North of Astrakhan the river banks keep low,

especially on the east side, where the land is a flat swamp cut by innumerable arms of the river, the water-edge being in great part reed-grown; the west bank, however, is a little higher, and is dry, and there are but few arms of the river, and little reed. The contrast between the two banks is thus so striking the whole way up that one cannot help believing there must be a definite cause. On this west bank, some 10 kilometres north of Astrakhan, the remains can still be found in the ground of the once so mighty Khazar capital, Itil, which for three centuries, down to 969, was the centre of their extensive dominion (cp. p. 214). Now in the neighbourhood is Kalmytski Bazar, the chief town of the Mongolian Buddhist Kalmucks, with a Buddhist temple.

It was growing dusk, and under the vault of the sky night swept over the broad, slow-moving face of the water; the low shores withdrew into the wavering darkness. From far off could be heard the crooning notes of the Volga's wonderful song of the Cossack robber-chief Stenka Razin, who was the friend of the poor and down-trodden, and who, when he found he was forgetting himself, his people, and his fighting out of love for the fair princess he had carried off from Persia, sacrificed her to the waters of the Volga, and then at the head of his men took Astrakhan (1670).

Volga, Volga, Mother Volga, take to thy bosom my lovely
    friend!
With one sweep he lifts her, while a star shot o'er the sky . . .
and thus does Stenka Razin cast his princess overboard.

Wherefore are ye silent, ye devils? Ho there, Filkan, dance
    me joy!
Play and sing, ye Don Cossacks! 'twill help her soul.
Forth from the sheltered order of the island out onto Volga's
    broad bosom
Steer fair painted ships in Stenka Razin's name.[1]

It is a curious thing that this name Volga, "Mother
Volga", which has so great a place in the life, the
thought, and the poetry of the whole Russian
people, is not Russian, but comes from the Finnish
people of the Bulgars, who founded a state on this
river already in the early centuries of our era.[2]
Their capital, Bulgar or Bolgar (= Volgar), afterwards gave the river its name. But before this it
was usually called Itil by the Tatars and Arabs,
after the Khazar town near the mouth, while
Ptolemy and the Greeks called it Rha, and the
Finnish tribes Rau.

Bulgar lay on the Volga near the Kazan of
today; and the ruins of the old capital are, it is
believed, at the village of Uspenskoye or Bolgar,
near Spask, about 25 kilometres below the mouth
of the Kama. In the early Middle Ages the whole
of the eastern part of the Russia of today from the
Khazar kingdom on the steppes in the south, along
the middle reaches of the Volga, and so northwards to the Finnish people of the Biarmians on
the White Sea—all this was occupied by Finnish-
Ugrians, and it was not until the 16th century

[1] After a translation by H. S. Schirmer.
[2] They were a part of the same people which at an early date made
its way west, and settled south of the mouth of the Danube,
becoming a serious danger for Byzantium. They gradually took over
the Slav tongue.

that the Slavs made a way eastwards and southwards along the Volga. After the power of the Khazars was broken in the south, and Itil lost its importance as a trading town, Bulgar became all the more important; and in the 10th century, when the Bulgars embraced Islam, it was a flourishing town, and the meeting-place for traders coming up the Volga even from Arabia, Persia, and Byzantium, and down the river from the north and west, even from Scandinavia. In A.D. 922 Ibn Fadhlân came there as envoy from the Khalif Al-Muktadir billáh in Baghdad. He has left a remarkable account of his stay.

For us northerners he is particularly interesting as telling us of his meeting with traders belonging to the *Rûs* people, who were from Scandinavia, and mostly Swedes; they founded the Russian State of Gardarike, having Novgorod for its capital.[1] This description of these forefathers of the Norwegians is one of the first known to us, but it is not altogether very flattering. "He saw the Rûs," says he, "as they came with their wares", and these were mainly skins and young girls. "They came from their land in their ships to Itil (that is, the Volga), and anchored there, and built themselves great wooden houses." What way they had come he does not

[1] Another Scandinavian-Russian State was, as is well known, founded in Kiev by the Varangians (in Russian = Varyagi), who evidently were both Norwegians and Swedes. Harold Hardrada was leader of the Varangians in Byzantium. It was the voyaging warrior Scandinavians who had the gift of leadership and could unite the land-tilling Slavs for warlike undertakings. There were so many of them on the Volga that they made incursions with their ships into the Caspian in the 10th century.

say; they may either have come down the river
from its upper part, or else from the Black Sea
up the Don, dragging the ships overland from the
Khazar town of Sarkel to the Volga, near the
Stalingrad (Tsaritsin) of today.

"Never have I seen such tall people," he says;
"they are as tall as palms, ruddy and red-cheeked.
They wear no undershirt and no caftan. The man
wears a coarse cloak, which he throws round one
side so that a hand is left free. Each man carries
an axe, a knife, and a sword. You never see them
without these weapons. . . . The women wear on
the breast a box made of iron, copper, silver, or gold;
to this a ring is fastened, and to this a knife. Around
the neck they wear chains of gold and silver, and the
number of these depends on the husband's wealth.
Their greatest ornaments are green glass beads.

They are the dirtiest people God ever made;
they never wash after the calls of nature, nor at
night. . . . They are just like wandering wild asses."
For an Arab, with his many prescribed ablutions,
anything of this kind was the most dreadful savagery.

We are told of their idols made of wood, and of
their offerings to them to be granted good trade.
In the houses each man had a broad bench on
which he sat with his girls and beauties that were
for sale. There he dallied with one of his girls, while
his friend, sometimes even several of the men at
the same time, looked on. . . .

There is a very remarkable account of a chief's
funeral witnessed by Ibn Fadhlân. The dead man,
wearing splendid apparel of gold cloth with gold
buttons and a gold cloth-cap edged with sable,

was on his ship, which was drawn ashore, seated on a bench spread with coverings of Grecian gold-cloth and pillows of the same cloths. His weapons were laid at his side, and intoxicating drink, fruit, bread, meat, and so on. A dog was cut up and thrown into the ship, as also two horses, two oxen, a cock, and a hen. They drank heavily, and "often one of them would die, beaker in hand". The girl who had agreed to follow the dead man, after much drink and debauchery, especially with six of his men, was killed on the ship by the death-angel, an old woman. At the end the dead man's nearest kindred walked backwards and naked up to the ship, and set fire to the wooden props underneath it. Everything was soon alight, and the chief with the girl took the long journey to the other world.

The Bulgar kingdom on the Volga was shaken to its foundations by the Mongol storm in the 13th century; it still kept its own nominal rulers, but was definitely destroyed by Tamerlane at the end of the 14th century. A little later its place was taken by the Tatar kingdom at Kazan, founded in 1437, which was in the end conquered by Ivan the Terrible in 1552. The way was now open for the Russians down the Volga, and in a few years they took the land to the south as far as Astrakhan and the Caspian Sea.

Thursday, the 14th of July. Steadily we went north along this mighty waterway, winding through the endless flat-land. On the low, swampy expanse to the east there was hardly a house or a village to see, but along the western bank there were many.

The heat was grilling, and even by night it was sultry in our berths. But what was worse was the gnats; there were a lot of them, and we knew that these bring malaria with them. But what can one do? If the windows are shut, the heat is unbearable; and if you open them, then the gnats come in. One ought to sleep under mosquito-nets.

Otherwise this is a splendid, lazy life; one can hardly think of a more beneficial rest than a journey like this on one of these fine boats up or down the Volga. From Astrakhan to Nizhni Novgorod is seven days, and the return journey is five. As you glide on over the broad waters, you see the life on this giant river gliding by you, the banks on both sides, the plains stretching inland, and the villages with the great white churches and their high domes; and you see the people working in the fields. At long intervals the ship ties up at some more important village or a town, and on the barge that makes the wharf you see peasants, grave men and women and young folk—of the South Russian type, darker than they are in the north, with a blending of Tatar, Finnish, Mongol, and other peoples. Near the shore their vehicles (*telegas*) stand. The flat steppe-land, stretching far away both east and west of this lower part of the Volga, is the abode of the Mongolian Kalmuks and their herds, and of the Kirghizes and Tatars.

On board there was a collection of people of many kinds. There were orthodox Soviet functionaries, full of enthusiasm for the revolution and the new model which is to bring Russia a new and great future. There were rather more lukewarm or doubting business men and merchants who were ready to believe that all might be well, if only they were allowed to carry on their business without interference by the authorities. There were others who were filled with bitter scorn for the whole system as an impossibility; and there were young married couples who had no thought for anything, whether red or white, revolution or anti-revolution —they had enough to think of with themselves and their own affairs. But all of them were taking their fill of this health-giving, lazy life under a cloudless sky in a peaceful world.

Among others there was an attractive young married couple, whom I got to know in spite of the language difficulty; they knew little of anything but Russian, of which, I am sorry to say, I was not master. The young wife had tuberculosis of the lungs, and they were now on their way up the Volga, and then up the Kama to Ufa and the Bashkir Republic, where she was to stay some time in the hope of finding a cure in the forest and mountain air. It was sad to see this young and lovely creature, still in the early summer of life, and to think that perhaps she might never come back this way again.

But, like life, the river flows ever on, without stop and without pity.

> Along Volga's broad bed
> the flood cleaves wide paths.
>
> .   .   .   .   .
>
> The eye searches o'er waves
> for well-known, beloved islands.

In the afternoon we went through a stretch of the river where there were great quantities of dead

fish floating everywhere, often tightly packed together. Unluckily I could not get any of them picked
up for me; but they looked to be of an ordinary,
middling size. What was the cause of all this
destruction I could not find out; but the captain
said that quantities of dead fish such as this were
sometimes to be seen in the Volga. It looked just
as if a great barge full of fish might have sunk,
and all the cargo have floated out of it. What
Professor Arvid Behning, director of the Volga
biological station at Saratov, tells me in answer to
my question is that there are two possibilities. It
may have been Volga herrings (*Caspialosa volgensis*),
which up to the end of June spawn in the lower
Volga up as far as Stalingrad (Tsaritsin, cp. p. 225).
They die wholesale after spawning, and it may be
that as late as the 14th of July we met with
these dead Volga herrings, though hardly likely
in such great, compact quantities. The other possibility is that it was a result of the fishing for freshwater fish ("white-fish", cp. p. 227), which starts
just at this time in the bays amd arms of the river.
It often happens then that the fishermen, through
lack of markets, or of salt, or for some such reason,
throw away great quantities of dead or spoilt fish into
the river. As there are great fisheries in the part we
were then in, near Cherny, it may well be that we met
with dead fish of this kind. In this case they would
mainly have been various kinds of bream (*Abramis
brama, A. sapa, A. ballerus*), blick (*Blicca björkna*), etc.
This agrees well with the look of the fish we saw floating, and this explanation seems the most likely one.

We came to the German town of Sarepta, which

right down to the end of the last century belonged to the Moravian Brothers. Instead of the widow's never-failing flour-bin and cruse of oil, this Sarepta is famous for its mustard. From here and a long way north past Saratov to Volsk there is along the east side of the Volga a line of German colonies with many villages, founded by Catherine II in the later 18th century. These colonists, who still speak pure German, are very good agriculturists.

Sixty kilometres east of Sarepta, on the other side of the many arms of the Volga, lies the village of Tsarev. Here stood earlier Sarai, where in the 13th century Batu, Chingis Khan's grandson, set up his golden tent, and it became the capital of the Mongols' Golden Horde, and their once so mighty state.

Some 30 kilometres farther north from Sarepta along the river, which here makes a great bend, lies Tsaritsin, now known as Stalingrad. It is hereabouts that the Don comes nearest to the Volga; the distance between them is about 50 kilometres, and here there was from olden times a porterage over to Sarkel, the strongly fortified Khazar town on the Don, which could be navigated down to the Black Sea.

It was most pleasant to come out onto the broad deck in the morning, greeted by bright sunshine and glittering water, and take one's coffee and breakfast as the land slipped by on both sides. The cooking on board was most excellent, and refreshments and meals could be ordered when we wished, and served up under the awning on deck. We invited the very pleasant captain to take his meals with us; he was a good seaman who had been taking these great boats up and down the river for many years, and he could tell us much about the life on the Volga both before and now. Before the World War there was a varied and lively world of travel here, with tourists to and from the East, the Caucasus, and Southern Russia. Eight great passenger-boats left Astrakhan for the north every day, besides the cargo-steamers; now there is only one, and a mixed cargo and passenger boat. After dinner there was coffee and a good cigar, while the sun sparkled on the water and parched the broad plain. It was a wonderful *dolce far niente*. And when darkness fell Russian music and song was heard from the great saloon, while water and plain lay dreaming under the starry vault.

> O—ho—hey, o—ho—hey
>
> .   .   .   .   .
>
> Volga, thou art deep and great,
> Volga, thou art mother of all.
> Ay da—da ay da, ay da—da ay da.
>
> .   .   .   .   .
>
> Volga, Volga, slow and long . . . "

From the moment we came into the Volga delta, as we have remarked more than once, it had been striking to see how the west bank of the river was always higher and steeper than the east one, which was everywhere quite low and sloped gradually into the water. It was most striking, too, as we have said, that the deepest and widest channel in the delta—the one we came up by—was for the whole way the westernmost of the arms of the delta. And so it was all the way to the north-west right up to Stalingrad (Tsaritsin), where the river makes a sharp bend from the north-east. All along this stretch of 450 kilometres the land on the east side of the main course of the river is quite low, flat, and swampy. Above Stalingrad the river throws off a side arm, the Akhtuba, which follows the eastern side of the main river channel, more or less parallel to it at a distance of 12 to 22 kilometres, right down as far as the lower and broader delta. The lowland between the two arms is cut through and overflowed by a tangled net of branches of the river, which when the floods are out puts most of this land under water for a breadth up to 30 kilometres or more. The width of the main river may be from 480 to 3,500 metres, with depths of over 25 metres.

Throughout the whole length from Astrakhan up to Sarepta the land behind the western, steeper bank is undoubtedly higher than that on the east side, but it likewise runs back flat; it is made up by loose, post-Tertiary deposits, while to the north it has ranges of hills consisting of layers of heavier rock from the Cretaceous and Tertiary periods. This characteristic feature—that the river banks are so much higher and steeper on the west side than on the east—became more and more striking as we went north. North from Stalingrad the west bank is 30–40 metres, being formed in great part of sandstone and limestone, and flinty clay (from the Cretaceous and Tertiary periods); while the east bank is low, quite level meadow-land, often traversed by arms of the river, as far north as the Kama and beyond, except for a short stretch by Samara, where the river forces its way through the Shiguli mountains, rising to 353 metres. It is also remarkable that most of the towns and larger villages along the lower Volga lie on the west bank, and the land there is thickly populated and has many villages, while that on the other side of the river, and far to the east, is low and flat with barren salt-steppes and a scantier population.

As I see it, there can be no doubt that these characteristic conditions must be set down to the effect of the earth's rotation, which in the Northern Hemisphere, where water is flowing south across the direction of this rotation, will divert it right-wards to the direction of the flow. This force of diversion brings it about that the stream in a broad river will usually be strongest along its right side,[1] and the flowing water will have its greatest erosive power on this side. It must be borne in mind that the power of flowing water to carry off gravel and stone increases as the rate of flow raised to the sixth. This means, therefore, that if the rate of flow is doubled, the water will be able to remove sixty-four times as large bits of gravel and stones. The river-bed will thus usually be deepest near the right bank, and the river will wear this bank more than the left one. In this way the river-bed will tend to shift all the time to the right. In a fairly flat land, especially if it is made up of loose layers easy for the river to wear, such a shifting, therefore, may go on at a relatively fast rate, and become of great importance. On the left side of the river there will then be a low flat land left behind, while the right bank grows higher and steeper as the river digs its way into higher land. This shifting of the river-bed over a plain of loose composition will take an even course until it is held up by ridges of heavier

[1] Cp. F. Nansen, *Gjennem Sibirien*, 1914, p. 128 f.

rock, and then the rate of erosion will be vastly slower.

As early as 1859 the Frenchman Babinet, and in 1860 the well-known Russian scientist von Baer, suggested the likelihood of this shifting of rivers owing to the earth's rotation. Many geographers and geologists have made the objection that the effect of this rotation on the course of rivers cannot be great enough to be perceptible, in comparison with the effects of so many other factors. But to me it seems quite beyond understanding that anyone who has seen the lower reaches of the Volga can still feel any doubt as to the great importance of this effect of the earth's rotation. Exactly the same striking features distinguishing the banks are found again in many other Russian rivers and the great rivers of Siberia, although seldom so clearly as here.

Much of the lowland left behind it to the east by the Volga as it has shifted westwards, land which is now in great part salt-steppes, was many thousand years ago covered by the Caspian Sea, since the level of this sea was for a long time higher, and it spread over an area many times greater than today. This was at a time when, as we said before (cp. p. 193), the precipitation in these parts was very much heavier in comparison with the evaporation than it is now. At this time, too, the volume of the Volga was probably greater. The water which now gathers on these plains all evaporates without finding any outflow, and as a result the surface of the ground becomes saturated with salt and barren, often being quite covered with a salt-crust.

The sharp bend of the Volga at Stalingrad and

Sarepta, where suddenly it bends away at a right-angle from the Iergeni hills (the Volga hills) on its right side, and flows away over the low flat steppe-land to the south-east, may probably also find its explanation in the fact that the Caspian throughout a considerable earlier period came as far as here. It is only a relatively short time that the river has been flowing in its present bed over the low plain down to the delta on the present coast of the sea;[1] but the time has been long enough for there to have arisen here also, as we have seen, a difference in height between the right and the left bank, although the land is flat everywhere; and the shift may well have been as great as would seem to be shown at the bank by the low swamp-land with the many side-channels which has been left behind by the river on the left side of its main channel.

In the districts north of Stalingrad (Tsaritsin) the soil is very fertile; the area of the so-called "black earth", in particular, stretches far to the west. This soil is so rich that, if there was always rain enough, it would yield quite extraordinary crops; but it is the rain that often miscarries, and of which there is seldom quite enough. And now, too, there was a brown and dried-up look over parts of the plain to the west. Although it is Russia's richest corn-land, in very rainless years there can be distress in these districts. So it was in 1921–2, when the drought brought about the great famine, and it was just here and north as far as

[1] Vertical movements of the earth's crust during and after the Ice Age may also have been of importance.

Samara and Simbirsk that its ravages were worst. Instead of corn being exported, it had at that time to be imported in great quantities. Under Mr. Hoover's lead much help was brought from America, and at the end meals were being given to 10 million people daily; we, too, in Europe did what we could to help.

The sun shines down overpoweringly from the cloudless sky, the villages smile peacefully in the warm summer, the churches gleam white against the blue high above the plain, and the peasants come in their jolting *telegas* to the great waterway —what a beautiful, soothing peace! But black shadows from that terror-stricken time cannot be driven away. These very villages were cities of death. In house after house the same dreadful sight of dying and dead wraiths of humanity. Parched grass and leaves, pounded bones and horses' hooves instead of bread. No fuel, so that the skeleton bodies froze fast to the ground ere life had left them. An awful house where those of the family still alive lay up on the great cold stove, so weak that they could not raise themselves—between them a new-born child, on the floor an old woman raking about in the fevered ravings of the last stage of spotted typhus; driven out of the other houses, she had found a last sanctuary here, whence they no longer had the strength to drive her. In a children's home forty-two died last night, and they still lay in the beds with the living beside them, who sat and gazed with the great wondering eyes of children on death, the great release from all suffering. Bodies were dug up from churchyards to be eaten. Parents, in their frenzy, killed their children to get food.

Over 30 million people were starving, and besides this epidemics swept them, worst of all, spotted typhus. Over three million died in spite of the help which came too late, and too little of it. And over these same plains thousands of wasted men and women fled, without food and not knowing whither —only to get away, away through the icy winter, while they and their last camels and horses fell dead along the frozen roads.

All traffic in the rivers stopped by the ice, the railways in confusion : the few trains that ran, overflowing with fugitives, came to a stop on the way; people died in the carriages. Horrors on every side.

And in past times? What cannot the history of these steppes relate of want, cruelty, changing fortunes? Host after host has marched over them, dealing death, destruction, and want: Huns, Avars, Pechenegs, Mongols, Turks, Tatars. And last came the civil war, and the great famine to end all. But in this tough, patient people's depths there still lie capabilities and forces as yet unused. In their wonderful music one feels as though from the echo of past sufferings, of great melancholy of the steppes, hope rises up for a day that is to dawn.

But now the journey was soon to end. On the 16th of July we reached Saratov; from here we were to take the train to Moscow, and so on to Norway. We had to say farewell to the Volga, and to the life on its slowly gliding waters. Through the steppe-land it flows on in summer's beauty and under winter's cloak, as that deep melancholy flows through the history of the Russian people.

INDEX

INDEX

Printed in the United States
111916LV00002B/73/A